200 English Grammar Mistakes!

A Workbook of Common Grammar and Punctuation Errors with Examples, Exercises and Solutions So You Never Make Them Again

MELONY JACOBS

TABLE OF CONTENTS

INTRODUCTION

The English language has its grammar outline. This outline is all about medium and convention that determines and guides how to speak and write. In grammar, this outline includes word spelling, word inflection, and word arrangement in sentence making. More importantly, English language is not static; rather, it is dynamic. The language has gone through various evolutions from the days of retaining German forms of the plural of some words until now. Therefore, communication requires adequate and proper understanding of grammar.

I am Melony Jacobs, a 52 years old professional editor and proofreader. I studied writing and the English language in the university. Hence, you can count on my experience and expertise to help to be more effective as a speaker and writer of one of the most popular languages in the world. I am committed to learning and that is why I read at least a book every week. I have come across many common mistakes people make when they speak and write.

Therefore, I have decided to contribute my quota to help others by putting this material together.

I am on a personal quest to help people improve their English grammar skills. I have written this book because I believe a book is the best way to put all the information together in a coherent manner. English grammar simply means how the English language is structured. It is a 'system' of how the English language is structured. It is very necessary that you develop a good grammar structure for many reasons. Some of the reasons are;

- ***To have clear communication***: Clear communication is fundamental as an individual. The biggest problem that arises from poor grammar is unclear communication. People tend to have incoherence in speeches simply because of grammatical blunder. If you make a mistake of including a singular verb where inappropriate, you may communicate a wrong message.

For example, if you are just deplaned and you say; "Our flight time **is** approximately forty-two minutes. " The person you're talking to may think you haven't boarded the plane at all. However, the correct thing to say is: Our flight time **was** approximately forty-two minutes. (Past tense)

- ***Wrong impression:*** Psychologists says; *"first impressions are lasting."* If you are a job applicant, the first thing you may want to take care of is your cover letter and curriculum vitae. For example, if the cover letter is an embodiment of grammatical mistakes, you may have practically created a wrong impression of yourself irrespective of how qualified you are for the job. Also, if you are preparing, or presenting a proposal for a project, you need to have a good command of English language to make sense to your audience.

Sometimes, there may be disagreements about what correct or incorrect English is. Incorrect grammar is commonly used in informal communication or speech. But, does that make it correct and appropriate? Correct grammar remains correct irrespective of where and how it is used (whether formally or informally), likewise incorrect grammar. Therefore, it is important that you strive to learn and be effective in the way you handle the English language. You should not stop learning. Hence, you need to leverage guide and outline that exposes your knowledge to grammar mistakes just like this book.

In this material, the errors are discussed by stating them with examples. Then, the correct versions are shown thereafter. It is important that you are able to consolidate what you are learning. Learning cannot be said to have taken place when you cannot recall the information. Any information that cannot be recalled is useless to you and others. To help you consolidate your learning so that you won't make the same errors again, there are multiple choice quiz questions in this material. After the correct versions have been highlighted, you will have multiple choice questions to answer to help you recall.

Foundational English grammar mistakes in various parts of speech are discussed in this book. In other words, you will learn to avoid basic mistakes when using verbs, nouns, adverbs, pronouns, and adjectives. There are also common mistakes people make when using grammar components like heteronyms, homographs, and homophones. You will get to know the correct way to go about the use of these grammar components as well and much more.

In the social media era, it has become much more important to be careful about the way you speak and write. Your mistakes can go viral all over the word in no time. It is not right to bully people and I will never advocate that. However, the reality is that there are unscrupulous people in this world who will pounce on the errors of others mercilessly. Hence, you need to protect yourself from being a prey to such mischievous people. Thankfully, you don't need any sophisticated weapon to protect yourself but adequate and constant learning.

Therefore, I encourage you to read this book with the desire to improve your grammar skills. When you improve your communication and writing skills, you are adding more value to yourself. Hence, don't read this book just because you are less busy and can't find something else to do with your time. Study it to get better and become more effective. I have done my part to put together accurate information in a coherent way to boost your effectiveness. The ball is in your court to play your part by studying the material with the right attitude. I know you will play your part. Let's get started!

FOUNDATIONAL/BASIC ENGLISH GRAMMAR MISTAKES

Every grammatical blunder in English language cannot be overlooked because they can be misleading. In this chapter, we will explore Basic English grammar mistakes and their correct versions. These errors have to do with wrong usage of different parts of speech such as verbs, pronouns, adjectives, and adverbs. Unlike other grammatical blunders, these mistakes are often obvious. People make such mistakes due to ignorance or negligence. However, mistakes remain what they are regardless of the reasons they occur.

Verbs

Verbs are simply action words that make your sentences meaningful. When using verbs, there are various forms to take note of.

Verb forms

For example;

Base form	S-form	Past form	ing-form	Past/passive participle
Play	Plays	Played	Playing	Played
Join	Joins	Joined	Joining	Joined
Find	Finds	Found	Finding	Found
Think	Thinks	Thought	Thinking	Thought
Discuss	Discusses	Discussed	Discussing	Discussed

e.g., pay attention to the following sentences used wrongly used.

Incorrect:	He **play** table tennis.
	He **steal** the bread.
	He **find** it difficult to solve.
Correct:	he **plays** table tennis.
	He **stole** the bread.
	He **found** it difficult to solve.

Remember: use an 'e' in the –ed (past simple and –ed form) of regular verbs. And, when you have regular verbs where vowel changes from 'i' to 'a' to 'u', use 'a'

in the past simple and 'u' in the '-ed' form.

Incorrect   she **enjoy** the movie.

I was very thirsty so I **drunk.**

Correct   she **enjoyed** the movie.

(past simple)

I was very thirsty so I **drank** water.

(past simple)

MCQs (choose the appropriate option from the following past simple forms)

1. The ship _______ before we got there. (A. had sink B. had sank C. had sunk)

Answer: C

2. The film _______ at 3pm. (A. began B. begun)

Answer: A

When using verbs, some forms may be used in more than one case

a.) Imperative use case such as when it begins a sentence in "play football with me." This makes a complete meaning on its own.

b.) Present tense use case such as "you play very well."**NOT** "you plays very well."

c.) infinitive use case such as "he'd like to play."**NOT** "he'd like playing."

In the above listed 'use cases,' any attempt to change the form of verb in the order of sentences will render the sentence incorrect.

Watch out for irregular verbs that have base form '-d' and past tense '-t' such as:

Incorrect	He **spend** millions of dollars on the surgery
Correct	He **spent** millions of dollars on the surgery

Do not use regular past simple '-ed' form for irregular verbs

Incorrect	He **spended** weeks before coming
Correct	he **spent** weeks before coming

Some prepositional words (e.g., about, for, and in) are not used with some verbs used in certain forms. E.g.

Incorrect   The school board **discussed about** expelling the student

Correct   The school board **discussed** expelling the student

There are prepositional words adequate with prepositional verbs. E.g., lies under, listen to, depend on, wait on, etc.

Incorrect   I like to **listen** him speak

Correct   I like to **listen to** him speak

Incorrect   He loves to **wait upon** his parents

Correct   He loves to **wait on** his parents

MCQs: choose the appropriate options from the statements below

1.   _______along with me (A. read B. reading C. is reading)

Answer: A

2.   He likes _______ (A. dancing B. dance)

Answer: A

3.   You should _______ the floor (A. scrubs B. scrub)

Answer: B

4.   I ____ he was coming yesterday (A. learned B. learnt C. was learning)

Answer: A

5.   She _______ my assistance on her assignment (A. request B. requested C. requested for)

Answer: B

6.   We _______ his appearance in court last week (A. demanded B. demanded for C. demand)

Answer: A

7.   We _______ God (depend, depending on, depend on)

Answer: A

Adverb

Adverbs are words that modify verbs, other adverbs or

adjectives. An adverb usually answers questions of 'what way', 'why', 'where' and 'when.' Some students often commit blunders when using adverbial words in statements. Study below important adverbial rules to follow when making sentences.

Adverbial use of ''very, much, so, and too''

'Much' is a comparative word and should be used in comparative degree and past participle tense

Incorrect	Joe is **more** taller than his sister
Correct	Joe is **much** taller than his sister

*Use adverb clause **'that'** with 'so' and 'too' with 'to' infinitive*

Incorrect	The lion is tough, other animals tremble at its roar
Correct	The lion is **so** tough **that** other animals tremble at its roar.

Incorrect	The candidate is **too** good for the job
Correct	The candidate is **too** good **to** do the job

*Two negative words from words such **as 'seldom, barely, never, often, merely, rarely, etc.'** should be avoided. Any of the categories can stand alone.*

Incorrect	Lisa **barely never** comes to class
Correct	Lisa **barely** comes to class

Incorrect	I **hardly don't** know anyone in the church
Correct	I **hardly** know anyone in the church

Remember: don't use any of the words with their negative meaning words.

The use of 'as;' Use adverb 'as' when introducing predicative verb words like know, describe, regard etc. Also, avoid using adverb 'as' when introducing predicative verb words such as choose, make, call etc.

Incorrect	He was described a bully
Correct	He was described **as** a bully

Incorrect	Albert Einstein is called **as** genius
Correct	Albert Einstein is called genius

When answering questions, 'yes' must go with affirmative responses, while 'no' must go with negative answers e.g.;

Incorrect   Have you eaten today?

                   No, I have eaten

Incorrect   Have you eaten today?

                   No, I have **not** eaten

Do not place adverbs of manner before intransitive verbs e.g.;

Incorrect   The lady **confidently** spoke to the tough guy

Correct   The lady spoke **confidently** to the tough guy

MCQs: choose the appropriate options from the statements below

Australia is a ______ beautiful country   (A. so B. very C. much)

Answer: B

I was forbidden ______ (A. 'not to go' B. 'to go,' C. 'never to go')

Answer: B

It appears this house is _____ bigger than the former house (A. more B. much C. very)

Answer: B

Cow milk is _____ nutritious   (A. too B. very C. much)

Answer: C

The student is _____brilliant _____ his teachers were proud of him (A. 'very, that' B. 'so, that')

Answer: B

He _____ comes late to meetings (A. often B. often always C. barely never)

Answer: A

Are you coming for the test?   (A. 'Yes, I am not coming' B. 'Yes, I am coming')

Answer: A

She _____________ (A. beautifully sang B. sang beautifully)

Answer: B

Adjectives

As a noun defines or names something, an adjective gives more information about a noun or pronoun. It can appear in regular, comparative or superlative forms. When qualifying, they come directly before the noun or pronoun being qualified. E.g. he is a **big** man. The word 'big' here, gives additional information on the noun 'man.'

Below are rules to pay rapt attention to avoid mistakes in adjective usage when making sentences.

Avoid using double comparatives in sentences e.g.,

Incorrect   James is **more bigger** than Joseph
Correct   James is **bigger than** Joseph

Adjective 'many' goes with countable nouns (e.g. miles, books, cars etc.) While, adjective 'much' goes with uncountable nouns (water, air). Also,' less' is used with uncountable nouns and 'fewer' is used with countable nouns.

Incorrect   There are **much** miles to cover in the race
Correct   There are **many** miles to cover in the race

Incorrect	The soup has **many** water
Correct	The soup has **much** water

Incorrect	I have **less** questions to go
Correct	I have **fewer** questions to go

Simply add '-er' as comparative to words like strong, fat, tall etc. e.g.,

Incorrect	And the boy grew **strong** and **strong**
Correct	And the boy grew **stronger** and **stronger**

Qualifiers such as 'both', 'all' must go before possessive words

Incorrect	He lost **his all** investment
Correct	He lost **all his** investment

Avoid mistakes of 'Farther' and 'further' in comparing distance

Incorrect	Which of the following places is **further?**
Correct	Which of the following places is **farther?**

The use of 'prefer'

Incorrect   I prefer biking **from** skating

Correct   I prefer biking **to** skating

Use superlative adjective (e.g., most) at the latter part of sentences such as we have in sentences like;

Incorrect   My brother is the **most** enterprising and ablest man I have seen

Correct   My brother is the ablest and **most** enterprising man I have seen

MCQs: choose the appropriate options from the statements below

1. Are your dresses ______? (A. Many B. much)

Answer: A

2. There is too ______ noise in the air (A. much B. many)

Answer: A

3. I have ___ worries than you do (A. less B. fewer)

Answer: B

4. We will go on ________ (A. next Friday B. Friday next)

Answer: B

5. ___ question in the script carries equal marks (A. every B. each)

Answer: B

6. Dad gave me _____ money to spend in school (A. little B. a little C. few D. small)

Answer: B

7. Tell me the ___ news (A. last B. latest)

Answer: B

8. The _____ of the story was emphasized (A. important B. importance)

Answer: B

Conjunctions

Conjunctions are words used to join 'a word to another word', 'a sentence to another sentence', and 'a word to a clause.' For example; he was playing music, yet I studied. Here, "he was playing music" is a sentence and "I studied" is another sentence. Word 'yet' is simply joining the two sentences together to pass key information in the compound sentence. There are several conjoining words that students commonly misuse in sentences. The following important rules are to be followed when using conjunctions.

Use 'not only' following 'but also'

Incorrect	He did **not only** slap her, he kicked her
Correct	Not **only did** he slap her, **but** also kicked her

The use of 'though and yet'

Incorrect	Although he studied hard, he failed
Correct	**Though** he studied hard, **yet** he failed

Avoid using 'not' with 'lest' because 'lest' is a negative word. When used, 'should' must follow.

Incorrect	You had better work hard **lest not** you become poor
Correct	You had better work hard **lest** you **should** become poor/lest you become poor.

In the absence of 'should' or shall, 'else' is appropriate. In essence, when you have 'will', would, or may instead of 'should' or 'shall', 'else' will replace 'lest'. E.g.,

Incorrect	Drive fast to the airport, **or else** you would miss your flight
Correct	Drive fast to the airport **else**, you would miss your flight

'Both' must carry 'and'

Incorrect	Both Jackson, Julian are together
Correct	**Both** Jackson **and** Julian are together

The use of 'other', 'rather' and 'than'

Incorrect	I would leave **than** sit here with you
Correct	I would **rather** leave **than** sit here with

you

Incorrect	**Than** sleeping late, I love studying
Correct	**Other than** sleeping late, I love studying

The use of conditional 'if' is different from 'whether.' This is because 'if' has a conditional connotation while, whether connotes uncertainty. E.g.

Incorrect	He doesn't come early, he will not be allowed entry
Correct	**If** he doesn't come early, he will not be allowed entry (conditional)

Incorrect	She likes it or not, she will be punished
Correct	**Whether** she likes it or not, she will be punished (certainty)

'Either or' and 'neither nor'

Incorrect	We came to the spa but we didn't meet Jane and John
Correct	We came to the spa but we met **neither** Jane nor John/we met **neither** of you

Incorrect	My client is not mad and not crazy, the lawyer said
Correct	My client is **neither** mad **nor** crazy, the lawyer said

Incorrect	I love taking ice-cream **or** yoghurt
Correct	I love taking **either** ice-cream **or** yoghurt

Incorrect	It is clear; you are telling a lie **or** saying the truth
Correct	It is clear; you are **either** telling a lie **or** saying the truth

Incorrect	**Neither** would he eat the food or let us eat it
Correct	**Neither** would he eat the food **nor** let us eat it

The use of 'such and that'; usually, 'such that' is used when in stating the extent or degree of something.

Incorrect	The rubber stretch that it broke
Correct	The rubber was stretched **such that** it broke

Incorrect	The stock market became flooded that it crashed
Correct	The stock market became flooded **such that** it crashed

Like is used to explain similarity and should be followed by a pronoun. Using 'as' it should be followed by a clause.

Incorrect	She sang alike **as** my sister
Correct	She sang **like** my sister

Incorrect	He was as bold **like** a lion
Correct	he was **as** bold **as** a lion

Incorrect	He ate like he was walking
Correct	He ate as he was walking

One conjoining word is enough to join two clauses successfully.

Incorrect	The director asked **that** what was his grade

Correct	The director asked **what his grade was**

Incorrect	He's often scared **that** he might repeat the course
Correct	He's often scared he **might repeat the course**

Incorrect	**Because** he wasn't quick enough, **therefore** we finished before him
Correct	**Because** he wasn't quick enough, we finished before him

Incorrect	He was angry. He slapped him
Correct	He was angry, **so** he slapped him

Incorrect	**Since** he is smart, **so** he always has his way
Correct	**Since** he is smart, he always has his way / he is smart, so he always has his way.

The use of 'so as' in a sentence usually is to indicate a purpose. So, when being used, be sure of the phrase that follows.

Incorrect He attending the gathering **so that** he can catch the perpetrators

Correct He attended the gathering **so as** to catch the perpetrators

MCQs: choose the appropriate options from the statements below

1. He had scarcely eaten__ (A. that his friend came B. when his friend came)

Answer: B

2. ___ did he help the poor kid, __ he took him home (A. not only/neither B. neither/nor B. not only/but also)

Answer: C

3. Read up ______ you should forget (A. or else B. lest C. else)

Answer: B

4. Bring me the report __ I forget (A. lest B. else)

Answer: A

5. He walked horridly ___ he would miss the bus (A. or else B. lest C. else)

Answer: C

6. ___ Jude ___ Martin are good English students (A. either/or B. both/and C. both/or)

Answer: B

Prepositions

To put in a simple way, propositions serve as linkers in sentences. A preposition is used to indicate relationship between nouns, phrases and/or pronouns. They are mostly very short words that stand in front of nouns. Also, they connect time, location, people, and objects when used in a sentence. Some of the examples are "of, to, under, in, into, with, etc." Preposition may be cumbersome to deal with in sentences. However, there are a few highlighted facts applicable that students may study as guide in acclimatizing themselves with prepositional words.

- In English language, there are more than one hundred propositions.

- Prepositions are generally followed by nouns and pronouns
- In making clear sentences, specific prepositions are required. That is to say that some prepositions are not always substitutable. E.g., the use of preposition 'in' may not work in the place of preposition 'on' in all cases.

Grammatical errors occur in the basic three types of preposition such as "preposition of time, place and direction."

Preposition of time

Prepositions in this category help to state when something had happened, has happened, or will happen. Examples of preposition of time are "at, on, in, before and after."

Abide by the following rules when using time preposition
Use preposition 'on' for days, and dates of the month

Incorrect   School resumes **in** Monday
Correct   School resumes **on** Monday

Incorrect   Christmas is **in** December 25th
Correct   Christmas is **on** December 25th

Incorrect	I got my birthday present **in** my birthday
Correct	I got my birthday present **on** my birthday

Use preposition 'in' when stating years, months, seasons, centuries and periods of the day.

Incorrect	My wife and I got married **on** 2002
Correct	My wife and I got married **in** 2002

Incorrect	Every year, my family vacation falls **on** spring
Correct	Every year, my family vacation falls **in** spring

Incorrect	Salvation came to us **on** the twentieth century
Correct	Salvation came to us **in** the twentieth century

Use 'at' when you have night, noon, and festive period.

Incorrect	We have our moments **in** the night
Correct	We have our moments **at** night

Incorrect	I go hiking **in** Christmas time
Correct	I go hiking **at** Christmas time

Incorrect	I will see you **in** noon
Correct	I will see you **at** noon

Use 'at' when you indicate exactness/accuracy e.g.,

Incorrect	The lines met **in** exactly 90 degrees
Correct	The lines met **at** exactly 90 degrees

Incorrect	We will see each other **in** 4pm
Correct	We will see each other **at** 4pm

Incorrect	His shift is **in** 3pm
Correct	His shift is **at** 3pm

Incorrect	We eat dinner **in** 7pm every night
Correct	We eat dinner **at** 7pm every night

Avoid wrong usage of other time prepositions such as "during, until, throughout, around and about."

Incorrect	The politician held the rally **around** the

	month
Correct	The politician held the rally **throughout** the month

Incorrect	The sun comes out **around** 6am every morning
Correct	The sun comes out **about** 6am every morning

Incorrect	He waited **till** he heard you had gone
Correct	He waited **until** he heard you had gone

Incorrect	He ran **round about** the circle
Correct	He ran **around** the circle

Incorrect	I met my wife **in** the holiday
Correct	I met my wife **during** the holiday

Preposition of Place

These are prepositions that indicate position. Avoid errors indicated from the following examples

Incorrect	There is something hanging **in** the wall

Correct   There is something hanging **on** the wall

Incorrect   There are images **in** the page
Correct   There are images **on** the page
Incorrect   Maxwell is **at** Dubai, visiting his niece **at** the hospital
Correct   Maxwell is **in** Dubai, visiting his niece **in** the hospital

Incorrect   I am **on** the crossroad
Correct   I am **at** the crossroad

Incorrect   Let us meet **in** the airport
Correct   Let us meet **at** the airport

Use 'inside' to indicate non-abstract positions and 'in' for abstract positions

Incorrect   The manual is locked **in** the car
Correct   The manual is locked **inside** the car

Incorrect   The fish is **in** the refrigerator
Correct   The fish is **inside** the refrigerator

Incorrect   I am living **inside** a province of Canada

Correct   I am living **in** a province of Canada

Preposition of direction

Avoid mixing prepositions such as "over, around and past"

Incorrect   Our horses run **across** the ranch every morning

Correct   Our horses run **around** the ranch every morning

Incorrect   That vehicle zoomed **passed** the truck

Correct   That vehicle zoomed **past** the truck

MCQs: choose the appropriate options from the statements below

He stepped ______ the house (A. out B. outside C. in)

Answer: B

He flew ____ of town (out, outside, away)

Answer: A

____the 30th of January marks our wedding anniversary (A. on B. in C. at)

Answer: A

We shall hangout _____ 6 o'clock tomorrow (A. on B. at C. in)

Answer: B

They'll meet ___ five minutes later (A. at B. in)

Answer: B

Noun

When you come in contact with the names of people, things (living or non-living things), countable and uncountable, then, you are talking about nouns.

Avoid the following fundamental and likely errors in nouns

Words like furniture, luggage, baggage, information, news, and advice are naturally singular

Incorrect   Please pack your baggages
Correct   Please pack your baggage

Incorrect   We are ready to receive **informations** on

the product

Correct   We are ready to receive **information** on the product

Incorrect   **These are the news** I love to hear

Correct   **This is the news** I love to hear

Incorrect   We are buying some **furnitures**

Correct   We are buying some **furniture**

Incorrect   Our government needs to care for the **poors**

Correct   Our government needs to care for the **poor**

Incorrect   Jesus fed the **blinds** with food

Correct   Jesus fed the **blind** with food

Incorrect   He said his **need** are numerous

Correct   He said his **needs** are numerous

Incorrect   Is there **breads** on the table?

Correct   Is there **bread** on the table?

Do not use 'brother' with 'cousin'

Incorrect	He's my **cousin brother**
Correct	He's my **cousin** (cousin is either male or female. 'He' already states the sex)

Incorrect	My friends **has** arrived
Correct	My friends **have** arrived

Incorrect	The counselor gave me some **advise**
Correct	The counselor gave me some **advice**

Incorrect	I've got **five dollars** note in my wallet
Correct	I've got **five dollar** note in my wallet

Incorrect	I have two dozens apple
Correct	I have two dozen apples

MCQs: choose the appropriate options from the statements below

Kindly put your _____ here (A. signature B. sign)

Answer: A

She is my _______ (A. cousin sister B. cousin)

Answer: B

He was my captain when I was in _____ (A. boarding B. boarding house C. board)

Answer: B

God can heal the _____ (A. deafs B. deaf)

Answer: B

The ___ here is not good enough (A. sceneries B. scenery)

Answer: B

Pronouns

Words used to avoid repetition of nouns are called pronouns.

Errors in pronouns may not appear common among English speakers, but the fact cannot be ruled out that for efficient communication, pronoun is a fundamental part of speech that has its errors among students or learners.

Pronoun errors occur in English when there is a

disagreement between the pronouns and the number of nouns. If noun is singular, the pronoun has to be singular and vice versa. Another way errors occur in pronouns is when the verb does not agree with the subject of the sentence. However, these two errors are intertwined.

Below are examples of common pronoun errors in grammar

The use of "one of, some of, and none of" must be taken with such that the verb agrees with the subject. Below, singular verbs 'eats, and was agrees with singular subjects

Incorrect	**One of** my course mates **eat** a lot
Correct	**One of** my course mates **eats** a lot
Incorrect	**Some of** the king's servant **is** here
Correct	**Some of** the king's servants **are** here
Incorrect	**None of** the athlete **were** around
Correct	**None of** the athletes **was** around
Incorrect	**Each boy** and each girl **were** given an exercise book
Correct	**Each boy** and each girl **was** given an exercise book

If the word 'one' is used in a sentence, you should use it throughout

Incorrect	**Someone** needs to work hard so that **someone** can make ends meet in life.
Correct	**One** needs to work hard so that **one** can make ends meet in life

Incorrect	**One** must take care of **himself**
Correct	**One** must take care of **oneself**

To avoid errors in pronouns, all transitive verbs such as "fill, enjoy, lend, give etc." must have an expressed subject in a sentence.

Incorrect	Elizabeth asked for her pen but she didn't give her
Correct	Elizabeth asked for her pen but she didn't give **it** to her

Incorrect	She drove the car to the gas station but the attendant refused to fill up
Correct	She drove the car to the gas station but the

attendant refused to fill **it** up

Avoid errors of using object in place of subject

Incorrect   In few weeks to come, my friend and **me** will be discussing the investment platform

Correct   In few weeks to come, my friend and **I** will be discussing the investment platform

Other common erroneous examples are;

Incorrect   It feels good spending time with **they** and their family

Correct   It feels good spending time with **them** and their family

Incorrect   Jane announced **she** and **her** son plans to leave the neighborhood next year

Correct   Jane announced **her** and **her** son plans to leave the neighborhood next year

Incorrect   Both my wife and **myself** felt so

	embarrassed at the situation we found them
Correct	Both my wife and **I** felt so embarrassed at the situation we found them

Incorrect	It was **me** who robbed the bank last week

Correct	It was **I** who robbed the bank week

Incorrect	Who is there? It is **me**
Correct	Who is there? It is **I**

MCQs: choose the appropriate options from the statements below

1. Mr. Lin followed __ and ___ son out of the grocery store (A. him/his B. he/his)

Answer: A

2. Alan then chased __ and __ daughter out of his house (A. her/her B. she/her C. he/him)

Answer: A

3. He gave ____ a good handshake after the presentation (A. he B. his C. him)

Answer: C

4. The man confessed it was ____ who raped the lady (A. him B. he C. his)

Answer: B

5. I have told ____ to move out (A. they B. them)

Answer: B

Interjections

Though not common among most academic writings, interjection has its significance in several other writings such as novels, fictional writings, emails and some other informal communication texts. Interjections are words used to indicate emotions such as surprise, love, hatred, anger etc. when used in sentences. They may appear either at the beginning, middle or end of a sentence conveying emotion.

The fact about interjections is that, even though they show emotions, *they are not grammatically related to the sentence.* Because interjections are expressed independently, serving an emotive purpose and followed by a sentence, there are usually no associated errors with them. However, interjections must agree with the purpose of sentences they are used for.

Avoid using contradiction between your sentence and the interjectory word

Incorrect   **hurray!** He broke his jaw

Correct   **What a shame!** He broke his jaw

Incorrect   **Bravo!** I'm not finished

Correct   **Alas!** I'm not finished

MCQs: choose the appropriate interjections from the statements below

_______ where is everyone (A. Why! B. Good work!)

Answer: A

We made it. ____ (A. What a pity! B. Wow!)

Answer: B

GRAMMAR COMPONENTS AND WORDS

As English language learners, there are Basic and complex English grammar errors made when communicating. To joggle your memory a bit; language use refers to your ability to effectively comprehend (when spoken or written to), produce (communicate) both spoken and written words. So, the understanding of how English language works is confined in thorough appropriation of English grammar rules which the English language lives by. As described in chapter one, there are Basic English grammar rules to abide with in order to communicate well. Any attempt to do otherwise would lead to a colossal grammatical error. In the same instance, other complex English grammar components and words also have specific rules to pay due respect to when being used, be it formally or informally. All said, let us go through the components and words.

Abbreviations

In a short sentence, an abbreviation (abbr.) is a chunk of lengthy phrases or words. As a user of English language, you can use an abbreviation when you need to reduce a large number of words in a sentence to a single reduced sequence of letters or to chunk an extensively long sentence into few letters to make your statement/sentence more interesting to read. For example, if you have to use North Atlantic Treaty Organization for every place you need to simply use NATO (an abbreviation); you'll realize how boring your writing can be to your audience. More important fact associated with abbreviations is that; they may communication easy for us. in this case, you don't have to write or speak ever word for every statement you mean e.g. "I am the CEO/CFO/MD of that company" looks cool right?

To clarify the concept of abbreviation; there are forms of abbreviation which are "acronym and initialism." An acronym is derived from the initial letters of a long word or phrase. When National Aeronautic Space Administration is reduced to NASA, it's simply an acronym. In acronym, you do not pronounce the acronym "letter for letter" rather; you take it as a single word.

NB. *Acronyms are pronounced as a word e.g. NATO (nar tow), NASA (narsar).*

Initialism is another version or form of abbreviation and it is derived when a phrase is reduced to initial letters. In this regard, initialized words are pronounced as individual letters. When you reduce National Football Academy to NFA, initialism is at work. Hence, initialized words are taken "letter-for-letter."

NB. *Initialism are pronounced letter for letter e.g. Personal Computer PC (peecee) NFA (en ef hey) Alternative Dispute Resolution (heydeearr).*

Whether you initialize or use acronym, abbreviating words can be erroneous if you do not acclimatize yourself to them.

Now that you know what abbreviation means and the varieties of abbreviation in the English grammar, let's go through common abbreviations and rules that need to be taken care of in order to avoid unnecessary errors.

You can abbreviate a word by omitting one or more

syllables e.g.

Examination	exam
Memorandum	memo
Decapitation	decap
Recapitulate	recap
Advertisement	advert

In the case of names, you can also omit one or more syllables e.g.

Fredrick	Fred
Jackson	Jack
Timothy	Tim
Rajji	Raj

Use cases of common written sentential abbreviations, pay attention to the following:

If in a sentence you mean to say "for example," simply use "e.g." 'E.g.' is initialized from the Latin phrase *'exempli gratia'* which in English is translated as 'for example.'

Also, do not confuse 'e.g. with i.e.'

As mentioned earlier, e.g. means for example, and it is used for sentence clarification by giving instances. 'I.e.' is from the Latin phrase *'id est'* as well translated as 'that is' or 'such that' in English. It is used to give more information or elaborate a sentence. However, these two ('i.e., and e.g.') may be used to clarify a sentence, i.e., by explaining the sentence more or by illustration and e.g. explaining by citing examples.

Illustrations;

Drinking and driving is dangerous **i.e.** the eyes become blurry, and the cognitive orientation is affected too.

Drinking and driving is dangerous, it can cause a lot of damages **e.g.** damage to you, damage to the environment where it happens.

To say **"take note"** or you want to draw readers' attention to an important aspect of your writing use **"P.S."**Although commonly used in corporate organizations to in memo and other messages, when used in non-corporate writings, "P.S." from the words **"post script"** is an effective abbreviation tool to communicate effectively.

Do not confuse abbreviation for these three words e.g. "they're, their, there"

Many a student make the error of using **"they're"** to mean

"they are" in English grammar. While that may look fancy or interesting, it is nonstandard to use. Desist from saying "they're coming" rather; use "they are coming."

Another error students make is deriving abbreviation **"ther're"** from **"there are."** Think about this; can "ther're" be substituted for "there are?" the answer is NO. It is nonstandard to use it in English grammar. If at all you wish to use an abbreviation from the word 'there,' a standard acceptable way is to shorten 'is.'
So instead of having **'there is,'** you can actually have **"there's."**

To avoid abbreviation errors when you are either writing or speaking, *you need to pay attention to the following commonly used abbreviations in English grammar:*

Use **'Mr. /Mr 'and Mrs./Mrs / Ms.** when you mean **'Mister or Missus'** respectively.

The idea behind abbreviated Mister/Missus with or without 'dot' connotation is that; 'Mr/Mrs' without 'dot' is acceptable in British English grammar while, Mr. / Mrs. Is acceptable in the American English grammar.

Abbreviate the word 'appointment' as 'appt.' and never mistake it for 'apt.' used for the word 'apartment.'

When you see **'misc.,'** it means 'Miscellaneous.'

'Tel.' implies **'Telephone.'**

'Est.' implies **'established.'**

Stop writing **'RSVP'** together; rather, you separate the letter by **'dot'** such as **R.S.V.P.** The popular initialism R.S.V.P is from the French phrase *"Repondez, s'ilvous plait"* used in inviting guest to occasions such as birthday parties and it simply to means "please reply or kindly reply" if you'll be present.

When you see **'Ave.'** certainly, **'Avenue'** is implied and it is similar to having **'Cyn.'** as **'Canyon.'**

Avoid writing **'BSC'** as the abbreviation for **'Bachelor of Science.'** This is absolutely 'wrong.' The only appropriate way to go about a standard abbreviation of this is by using **BSc/BS**. Whichever you use here is simply perfect.

MCQs: find the appropriate abbreviations for the following

1. And so on / and lots more
   A. Etc.

B. id est

Answer: A

2. Take note/please note

A. e.g.

B. N.B

Answer: B

3. Abbreviation to mean 'namely' is

A. Vice versa

B. Viz

Answer: B

4. Page thirteen means

A. P38

B. p.13

Answer: B

5. Compact disc read only memory

A. CD ROM

B. CD-ROM

Answer: B

6.   Universal Serial Bus

   A.   UnSB

   B.   U.S.B

   C.   USB

Answer: C

Homonyms, Homophones, Homographs And Heteronyms

The joy of every communicator in English language lies in getting the right information to the audience with the use of the appropriate words and appropriate in intention. To be an effective communicator, you must have a solid command of words to use in various contexts. You must acclimatize yourself with a variety of word meaning, spelling and how they can function effectively in sentences. This idea of knowing the means and spelling of words and what they mean in sentences brings us to the topic of homonyms.

Homonyms

Homonyms refer to those words that are spelt differently but sound similar and have different meanings. Even native English language speakers agree that English language has a lot of confusing words with similar sound when heard or pronounced. However, it is interesting to know that many of those words have different spellings. You should avoid the error of confusing words to mean distinctive meanings in your sentences so, pay attention to the grammatical errors that students and writers often make when using homonyms in English language.

Confusion with the use of Loose/lose

This is one of the most commonly confused homonyms among English speakers. "loose" simply means not bound together. It can also mean not firm or tightly fitted to something. While, "lose" means to be without, deprived of, or stop having.

An example of appropriateness of the words includes;

Incorrect   I am afraid I might **loose** you.

                        His pant is **lose**.

Correct   I am afraid I might **lose** you.

His pant is **loose.**

Confusion with their/there

Another blunder common to students lie in this category. It is almost difficult to identify in speech but the error is always open when discovered as written statements.

"Their" is used as a possessive word. It means belonging to someone or them. While, "there" is used to mean position, state, etc.

Example

Incorrect   The man was killed over **their.**

                   These are **there** books.

Correct   the man was killed over **there.**

                   These are **their** books.

Confusion with Your/ You're

The same error happens as it is for their/there explained

earlier. Just like "their," "Your" is used as a possessive word. While, "You're" is simply derived from "You are" (like an abbreviation).

Illustration;

Incorrect   **Your** at the edge of **you're** paradise today because you have worked hard in the past. **Your** innocent, and I know that.

Correct   **You're** at the edge of **your** career today because you have worked hard in the past. **You're** innocent, and I know that

Remember: to know if you are making the right sentences with the words, ensure you cross-check by replacing the words alternatively. To a large extent, by alternating the words, you're good to go. Whether you want to use "their, there, your and you're," an alternation of the polar word (e.g. your for you're) will be good for you to determine which is correct to use.

Confusion with Raw / Roar

These two words are very identical in pronunciation just like others. The distinctive difference is that; "raw" refers to unprocessed state of something i.e. uncooked. It may also mean "not organized or new something." "Roar" is referred to as a loud noise made by a lion or a machine engine.

Examples include:

Incorrect   The statistical table was made using **roar** data

The guy could **raw** to make the room shake

Correct   The statistical table was made using **raw** data

The guy could **roar** to make the room shake

The confusion with Dearth /Death

Dearth simply means the scarcity of something. It can also mean insufficient. A dearth of something means that thing is not enough. Death is entirely different and it means loss of life.

Incorrect   The prosecutor dropped the

charges because there was a death of evidence.

He was put to **dearth** by hanging.

Correct   The prosecutor dropped the charges because there was a dearth of evidence.

He was out to **death** by hanging.

The confusion with Bare / Bear

Bare simply means without appropriate something. "I killed the lion with my **bare** hands" means" *I killed the lion without using anything like gun or other objects.* "

Bear can mean an animal. It can also mean to "carry something" or "tolerate something or someone." Its past tense is "bore." The food in the barn belongs to the "bear" (talking about animal). "He asked her to bear with him" (talking about tolerate).

Incorrect   The man can on coal on **bear** foot.
                   It's really hard **bare** the burden of four kids alone.

Correct   The man can walk on coal on **bare** foot.
                   It's really hard to **bear** the burden of raising four kids alone

The confusion with Dare / Dear

Dear is used regarding affection or to mean intimacy. In contrast, **"Dare"** can be used in the form of challenge.

Incorrect — My ex-boyfriend was so **dare** to me that I felt disappointed when he cheated on me. He **deared** me to slap the soldier and I did it gladly.

Correct — My ex-boyfriend was so **dear** to me that I felt disappointed when he cheated on me. He **dared** me to slap the soldier's face, and I did it gladly.

Avoid the error of One's / Once

"One's and "Once" are similarly interesting words among users in this present age, and a lot of writers find it difficult to use appropriately because of lack of knowledge to distinguish between the two.

By simple analogy, "one's" is used as a possessive word. Just like you say the book is "his," "one's" can also be used in the same context. Further, when you use "one's" in a sentence, you are using it in a non-directional manner. For examples, you can say "it's good to take care of one's health;" instead of saying "it is good to take care of your health." In this way, you are saying people or humans should take care of their health and not necessarily referring to a specific individual.

"Once" is another case word and it means "a single time," "on a one time occasion or formerly." When you are using this word as compared to its counterpart, you are mentioning a single event of occurrence or a former event that had occurred.

For example

Incorrect	He was **one's** an elementary school teacher before he realized politics was his true dream.
	The flat mates saw each other **one's** every three months, yet they quarreled like cat and mouse.
	It is more important to purse **once** dream in life else, one would be not be satisfied in life.

I believe **once** family is more important than the billions of dollars to be made from billions trips.

Correct   He was **once** an elementary school teacher before he realized politics was his true dream.

The flat mates saw each other **once** in every three months, yet they quarreled like cat and mouse.

It is important that one pursue **one's** dream in life else, one would not be satisfied in life.

I believe **one's** family is more important than the billions of dollars to be made from business trips.

Avoid the error of Too / Two

This basically is an example of homophone. As a learner, it is useful to get used to word inflexions such as knowing that the word "too" is used in a sentence to "emphasize." It can also be used instead of word like "very, and also" such as, "we walked too/very slow and missed the bus." Another case is to say "I'd like to shake hands with Donald Trump too/also."

Word "two" is separate. Two is a number or a figure expressed in words. You should never substitute "too" for "two" in a sentence.

Examples

Incorrect

Mark my words, the **too** men are to blame if he doesn't come.
It is uncertain if I'll like to go **two.**

Correct

It is uncertain if I'll like to go **too.**
Mark my words; the **two** men are to blame if he doesn't come.

Through / threw

This can be confusing at times if you don't know which word is appropriate for a particular sentence. Actually, where confusion lies in these two words is in the '-th" pronunciation and this shouldn't be a problem anymore once you can familiarize yourself with the words now.

Incorrect   The dog went **threw** the doorway and attacked the man.

He couldn't bear the pain any longer, so he **through** the infinity stone away

I thank God for all his has brought me **threw**

Correct   The dog went **through** the doorway and attacked the old man.

He couldn't bear the pain any longer, so he **threw** the infinity stone away.

I thank God for all he has brought me **through**.

Avoid the errors accrue to Waist / Waste

"Waist" is simply below your ribs, and "Waste" means to be extravagant, or squander something whether you are accountable for it or not.

Incorrect   He didn't know swinging with the **waste** was a bad idea for male participants.

It was futile chasing the thief since we knew we would **waist** our bullets.

Correct   It was futile chasing the thief since we knew we would **waste** our bullets.

He didn't know swinging with the **waist** was a bad idea for male participants in the competition.

Avoid the errors of Toe / Tow

The "toe" is a member of your foot, and "tow" is to use a vehicle, helicopter, or boat to pull another boat, or vehicle or helicopter along.

Incorrect   There is a perfect way to **toe** your vehicle if you don't know.
Dermatologists often say you should care for your **tow** nails neat as much as you care for your face.

Correct   There is a perfect way to **tow** your vehicle if you don't know.
Dermatologists often say you should care for your **toe** nails neat as much as you care for your face.

The confusion of Tail/ Tale

Tail is usually a word related to animals, coin, and the word "tale" is a story that is imagined or true.

Incorrect   When you flip a coin, you'll get either head or **tale**.

                    Have you read the book called the **tail** of Lady Bug?

Correct   When you flip a coin, you'll get either head or **tail**.

                    Have you read the book called the **tale** of Lady Bug?

Avoid the mistakes of Red / Read

The word "READ" retains its spelling in present tense, past tense. But, "red" is primarily a colour, and it may connote danger. In this case, the past tense of read is compared to red because of the pronunciation.

Incorrect   On Tuesday afternoon, an accident occurred because, the **read** light was difficult to detect if it was damaged or working.

Daniel **red** the inscription aloud

Correct   On Tuesday afternoon, an accident occurred because, the **red** light was difficult to detect if it was damaged or working.

Daniel **read** the inscription aloud. (Past tense)

MCQs: find the appropriate answer to the following questions.

1. You _____ should come along
   A. Too/two
   B. Too/many
   C. Two/much

Answer: A

2. I told him to _____ me a letter
   A. write
   B. right
   C. wright

Answer: A

3. I love to ______ him speak.

    A. Hear

    B. Here

Answer: A

4. Villagers declare war on the ______

    A. Which

    B. Witch

Answer: B

5. That is the ____ we use in making bread

    A. Flour

    B. Flower

Answer: A

Homographs

Among the varieties of homonyms is homograph. By definition, homographs are words with the same spelling but have different meaning. Homographic words are mostly not pronounced the same way. Pay rapt attention to the following words and study their other meanings extensively. By doing that, you will be able to appropriate the "right" not "write" usage of each other words when you intent to use them again.

"Tear" /"Tear"

The word "tear" can mean water droplets from the eyes when crying. It can also mean to destroy a piece of paper into pieces. However, how the word is used in sentences and the appropriateness of the word in sentences is important for learners to know. You know which "tear" to refer to when writing sentences. You should also remember that "tear" meaning water drops from the eye when crying is a "noun" while, the second "tear" meaning ripping paper into pieces is used as a "verb." So, when they are used, you've got to be careful how noun words and verb words are used.

Examples: 1. He keeps shedding **tears** because his heart is broken.

2. I'll watch how to **tear** the robot apart without damaging its engine on YouTube.

"Bow / Bow"

When you hear "give me the bow" and "give a Taichi bow to the master," what comes to your mind? First, the first statement is meaningful based on the fact that "give me the bow" sounds like you are being told to hand over an object (bow (a weapon for shooting arrow)). The second statement "give a Taichi bow to the master" is also meaningful in the context that you are to demonstrate something (bow (bend forward at the waist to show respect to the master)). Either way, messages are being passed across. This requires the noun and verb practice as well as how they are pronounced which shows in the noun and verb forms as well.

Examples: 1. The three Hebrew men refused to **bow** to the gods of the land (verb – action).

2. The archery company that specializes in making **bow** is in Los Angeles (noun – bow as something made).

"Capital / Capital"

This homographic word should not scare you as a learner who's ready to gain knowledge on English grammar skills. One, capital can be a federal city. Two, capital can be used as a legal term to mean punishment. In these cases, the word is serving the noun function which may be confusing to you; but, you have to understand the context of the word usage.

Illustrations:

1. His crime was so great that his retribution was **capital.** NB: retribution means punishment for criminal act and the word "capital" there means "punishment by death."
2. Death by lethal injection should be the **capital** punishment for rape around the globe.
3. Did you know Atlanta is the **capital** of Georgia?
4. I doubt Mexico is the **capital** of all drug cartels in the world.

"Paste / Paste"

Paste is a mixture of content or a processed content e.g. tomato paste. In contrast, paste can mean to put a thing on another or glue something to the wall.

Examples;

1. Kindly pass me the **paste** to add to the sauce.
2. Melisa was bitter because the art design she **paste**d on the school board was removed by the arrogant classmate or hers.

"Lead / Lead"

Lead is a metallic material and also can mean show someone a destination. However, the past tense of lead is "led." Therefore, do not make the mistake of misrepresentation when using the word "lead" in sentences.

Examples:

1. The engineer could not use the **lead** due to the fault detected when he test-ran it.
2. He asked if the idea would not **lead** them into temptation.

"Rose / Rose"

Rose can either be the name of a person, colour or the name of type of flower. Also, it can serve as the past tense of rise.

Examples;

1. He **rose** in the morning and began to shout as he jumped and smiled at the same (the statement appeared he was schizophrenic right?).

2. Every name does not appeal to me, but when I hear **Rose,** my soul is lifted.

"Canvass/ Canvas"

Let's get a mix of art terminology and regular English grammar using "canvass and canvas." These can be very confusing as homographic words in English grammar. Simply put, canvass is verb, and it means to seek support or help or agreement on something. Canvas on the other end, is a kind of cotton, or linen clothing material.

Examples:

1. This is what most politicians do when it's time for campaign; they **canvass** for support.

2. Most art works I love most are made on **canvas.**

MCQs: find the appropriate answer for the following

1. Votes are got based on how you can ______
   A. Canvas
   B. Canvass
   C. Converse

Answer: B

2. It is hard to determine if the price of goods is ____
   A. fare
   B. fair
   C. fear

Answer: B

3. Can you please tell the ______ to come in?
   A. pear
   B. pair
   C. pare

Answer: B

4. We are not sure he will _____ them there

    A. leed

    B. lead

    C. led

Answer: B

5. it is difficult for saints to _____

    A. lye

    B. lie

Answer: B

PUNCTUATION MARKS

Among common grammatical errors in English language, punctuation errors are the most common. If you are not a good reader, you might not be able to detect the blunders. Punctuation implies using spacing, signs, and some other symbols with the intention of making readers understand either spoken or written texts. When you communicate, punctuation marks enable you to appear like an expert. Whether you are speaking or writing, there is always a need to punctuate. In fact, English grammar isn't complete without punctuation marks. Let's have some simple illustrations.

1. Since the launch of Ruger 57 other critical reviews have it that Ruger 57 Company has not only fulfilled its mission but has also overtaken its competitors in the handguns market thanks to its outstanding innovation and development invested.

2. "Since the launch of Ruger 57, other critical reviews have it that Ruger 57 Company has not only fulfilled its mission, but has also overtaken its competitors in the handguns market – thanks to its outstanding innovation and development invested."

3. "In the beginning was the word the word was with God and the word was God."

4. "In the beginning was the word, the word was with God, and the word was God."

If you are not a good reader, you might not be able to make sense of what is written in the first and third paragraphs. And now, when you read the second and fourth paragraphs, you'd realize that you could decipher the paragraphs easily and make sense of what is written. Your ability to do this is credited to punctuation at work in the paragraphs.

Another fact about punctuation is that; it helps you to make diverse meanings from a sentence. A popular example will give you a clear meaning here:

A plain text without punctuation

Given the statement, "Woman without her man is

nothing." This appears ambiguous, right? Let's look at the punctuated texts below:

"Woman without her man, is nothing." (Meaning that men are important to women)

"Woman; without her, man is nothing." (Meaning that women are important to men)

The above mentioned illustration simply helps to know that punctuations can help to differentiate meanings from words joined together to make sentences. Without punctuation, you won't know exactly what the statement is talking about.

All well said, there are about several punctuation marks commonly used in English grammar. The commonly used ones are explained in this chapter:

a. Period (also known as full stop)

b. Semicolon

c. Colon

d. Dash

e. Hyphen

f. Exclamation marks

g. Quotation marks

h. Apostrophe

i. Ellipsis

j. Comma

k. Question mark

Simply following the right and appropriate use of these punctuation marks will enable you to make good sentences and communicate effectively when writing.

Period (.)

Period is what people call "full stop." After you are done writing a complete statement or sentence, it should end with "period." Also, "period" one of the three punctuation marks used in ending sentences. An important thing you should know about the "period" is that; irrespective of the number of abbreviations used in a sentence, "period" must always come last, being the final stop. There are a few rules to follow so as to avoid errors when using period.

Do not add another period to a sentence ending already with a period.

If you have an abbreviation as the last word in a sentence, an additional period will make the sentence erroneous. This is because, initialized words e.g., O.C.P.D., are already making use of periods (dots) to separate the letters standing for each initial words. So, you must avoid adding an extra period when the last letter is already carrying a period.

Incorrect   Kindly wait for him He'll catch up with you..

                 I am the new C.M.D..

Correct   Kindly wait for him. He'll catch up with you.

                 I am the new C.M.D.

A period is meant to be added after a complete sentence has been made.

This rule is also important if you want to appear proficient in writing. Imagine you are talking, and you do not complete a sentence before progressing to another, that will make your listeners think something is wrong or you probably don't know what you want to say exactly. By not adding an ending punctuation mark like period to your sentence, simply makes it incomplete. Never leave out a period to conclude your sentence.

Incorrect   Nothing is as sweet as eating a candy

Correct   Nothing is as sweet as eating a candy.

For indirect questions, ensure you apply period.

People often omit the period to end indirect questions. Indirect questions are statements made by third persons. For example;

Jade >>>>>>>>>>>>>>>>>>>>>>>→Jude

> Jade: Where was the money? (Direct question)

Joan >>>>>>>>>>>>>>>>>>>>>→John

> **Jade asked Jude where the money was. (Indirect question)**

In this case, avoid using contradictory punctuation mark; rather, use period to end the statement.

Exclamation (!)

This is mostly used in story books, novels and other literature texts. It's rare to find exclamation marks in formal texts, publications, reports and some others. However, *exclamation marks are part of the verbal statements we make daily*. When you, out of surprise, say "Wow," what you have done simply shows an exclamation (i.e., how surprised or flabbergasted you are). So, by definition, exclamation marks are used to indicate surprise and emphasis in sentences. Also, Exclamations points are those marks that conclude interjectory words in English grammar. Check out the illustrations below:

> I am so disappointed in your attitude!
>
> Yeah, we won!
>
> You came? Wow!
>
> I am simply the best!
>
> I repeat; it's my time to reign!

Never use exclamation marks in formal writings. Don't forget this have been mentioned earlier; exclamation marks mostly appear in informal or conversational writing.

Ellipsis (…)

Ellipsis is used by prolific English language writers. It is a special kind of punctuation because of the beauty it adds to sentences and paragraphs as a whole. If you desire to omit a word, short paragraph, phrase or line of statement from a passage, ellipsis is the right punctuation mark for such purpose. Another interesting fact about ellipses is that; it makes your readers inquisitive of your paragraph. Readers become more interested in finding out more about the omitted part of the sentence or paragraph you are talking about.

Popularly, ellipsis uses just *three dots (three periods)*. Although, some other scholarly books may use more than three dots, the most appropriate number of dots applied in creating an ellipsis is three. Take note of the errors to avoid when using ellipsis in the below illustrations:

If you are omitting sentences or words in the middle or between sentences, use ellipsis.

Full statement

"I am a man of virtue leaving no stone unturned, lest I lose my heritage."

Ellipsis written:

"I am a man of virtue leaving no stone unturned…"

When applying the appropriate ellipsis, you should leave out punctuation marks like comma.

Let's evaluate this rule using the excerpt from Abraham Lincoln address to the Americans during the period of mass protests and upheaval of racism and discrimination in America.

The full text says

"Four scores and seven years ago, our father brought

forth, upon this continent, a new nation, conceived in liberty, and dedicated to the proposition that all men are created equal."

Ellipsis rewritten:

"…our fathers brought forth…a new nation…dedicated to the proposition…"

Comma (,)

Comma is simply a "pause" in a sentence. It is also used to join words or sentences together. You should also know that "comma" can sometimes serve the function of conjunction "and" in a sentence. Many ways to avoid comma errors will be shown you as you read further. Also, the use cases to perfectly punctuate your writing with comma will be explained and detailed as you read on.

Ensure to use comma to make your statement clearer.

Perhaps, you have groups and different categories of words, use comma for separation in order to avoid confusing the readers.

Incorrect: The money was shared among his wife

mother children company staff and other relatives.

Correct   The money was shared among his wife, mother, children, company staff, and other relatives.

*Simply use comma instead of using conjunction "and" between **two** adjectives.*

Although, using "and" isn't a bad idea; but, using comma makes your writing eloquent and intelligent.

Incorrect   On my way to the groceries yesterday, I met a **tattered** and **grievous** man.

                 Julius Caesar was a **mighty** and **influential** man in his time.

Correct   On my way to the groceries yesterday, I met **a tattered, grievous** man.

                 Julius Caesar was a **mighty, influential** man in his time.

If you have the name or title of a person in a sentence, use comma before or after the name or title.

Incorrect   Do you Dan think he will come?

Will he the CEO appear in court tomorrow?

Would you pass me the salt? Yes Mr., I will.

Correct   Do you, Dan, think he will come?

Will he, the CEO, appear in court tomorrow?

Would you pass me the salt? Yes, Uncle, I will.

Looking at the sentences above, you'd discover that the comma in "do you, Dan…" helps to make a clear, direct question to Dan specifically, if "he thinks he will come."Likewise the second statement "will he, the CEO…" helps to let the listener know that the person to "appear in court tomorrow," is the CEO.

Avoid making comma errors when separating the calendar

days, months and years and country.

Incorrect

My girlfriend and I met on July 15 1980 at the train station.

My mum and I are going to have our vacation on 15th May 2020 in Dubai UAE.

Correct

My girlfriend and I met on July 15, 1980, at the train station.

My mum and I are going to have our vacation on 15[th]May, 2020, in Dubai, U.A.E.

Avoid using comma if you are omitting any part of the date in a sentence.

Incorrect

My grandpa died in October, last year.

They should travel in November, 2020.

Correct

My grandpa died in October last year.

They should travel in November 2020.

If you have compound sentences, use comma to separate each sentence to have a clearer meaning.

Incorrect   Although he was not in class he did his best in the class work.

He was even though you didn't notice the best candidate for the job.

Correct   Although he was not in class, he did his best in the class work.

He was, even though you didn't notice, the best candidate for the job.

Use a comma when you have two or more independent clauses.

Incorrect   He quarreled with his wife before leaving home drove to his friend's house and went to the club.

Correct   He quarreled with his wife before leaving home, drove to his friend's house, and went to the bar.

Avoid using comma when you have "and" conjoining only two words, or entities.

Incorrect   You may share the fruits between her, and him.

Correct   You may share the fruits between her and him.

The only situation you may use comma before "and" is in a compound independent sentence of at least three clauses.

Incorrect   Barrister Mike was a great man he was a magician a father of three kids and was loved by many.

Correct   Barrister Mike was a great man, he was a magician, a father of three kids, **and** was loved by many.

Use comma when giving more details about someone or something. Please pay attention to the errors students make, and learn the appropriate way in the sentences below.

Incorrect   John the beloved who followed his master everywhere is in our midst.

Mr. James the ruthless soldier was assassinated during the coup d'état.

Apostle Paul who persecuted the Christians eventually became a hardened preacher of the gospel of Jesus Christ.

Correct John, the beloved, who followed his master everywhere, is in our midst.

Mr. James, the ruthless soldier, was assassinated during the coup d'état.

Apostle Paul, who persecuted the Christians, eventually became a hardened preacher of the gospel of Jesus Christ.

Apply comma to separate a question from a statement referring to the same thing. Many students often commit this error as well. Rather than including a comma, they use "period" instead, and that is erroneous.

Incorrect to say He couldn't go. Could he?

I can eat my cake now. Can I?

You can't eat your cake and have

it at the same time. Can you?

Correct   He couldn't go, could he?

I can eat my cake now, can I?

You can't eat your cake and have it at the same time, can you?

Use comma immediately after words such as therefore, so, however, moreover, hence, thereafter, etc. when used in sentences.

Incorrect   I will not pursue him for the money, moreover I still have his car with me.

He observed for several hours and thereafter began to dance.

She'd been smiling at me for about 45 minutes; so I approached her to know if we had met before.

Correct   I will not pursue him for the money; moreover, I still have his car with me.

He observed for several hours, and

thereafter, began to dance.

She'd been smiling at me for about 45 minutes; so, I approached her to know if we had met before.

Colon (:)

Colon is another kind of punctuation mark that many learners and writers leave out when writing in English language. It is not so uncommon that some articles rarely have elements of punctuation marks like colon, and that is why you need to learn how it functions, also learn the errors to avoid when using colons in sentences. Technically, colon is used to explain or give a list the same ways e.g., i.e., and namely are used in sentences. So, pay attention to the illustrations in the rules below.

For official letter writing, *use colon following salutation even if you are addressing the letter to the person by the first name.* This is in contrast to writing an informal letter where "comma" is used because the person being addressed is familiar. Although, many writers are often confused about making distinctions between which one to use between colon and comma; that doesn't mean it is appropriate to keep the confusion going. Now that you are inclined about the differences, ensure you make use of it.

For example: Dear Mr. Matthew:

Distinguished Senator:

Dear Ms. Melisa:

In the absence of introductory words like "for example," and so on, use colon.

Correct   Three things can make a man happy: good job, good wife, and amazing children.

We need a candidate with the qualities of: knowledge of Microsoft Office Access, R programming software and critical reasoning skills.

Do not use a colon if it does not follow a complete statement.

For example:

Incorrect   If you want your readers to understand your content, and ensure your supervisor awards you a good grade, you should : (1)

write legibly, (2) support your points with facts, and (3) cite relevant examples.

Correct

If you want your readers to understand your content, and ensure your supervisor awards you a good grade, you should (1) write legibly, (2) support your points with facts, and (3) cite relevant examples.

You can use colon to replace a semicolon when you have two clauses with one clause explaining the other without the use of conjunction "and."

I love vacations: traveling to Paris in France is my favorite.

In a sentence, *if just a clause follows the colon, do not capitalize the first letter immediately after the colon.* But if there are more than two sentences still explaining the same point and not joined with a conjunction, you should capitalize the first letter immediately after the colon and also capitalize the sentence next. Check the examples below;

He just realized after a decade, how bad he

is at mathematics: **he** doesn't know what one plus one equal to.

He just realized after a decade, how bad his spoken English had been: **He** doesn't understand why "give him him book" is wrong and "give her her book" is right. **He** also doesn't know the rules guiding the use of period in English grammar.

Semicolon (;)

It is similar in usage as the colon to a large extent, but the use cases of the semicolon is limited. Read on to get the errors.

Use the semicolon before words like; for example, therefore, i.e., however, when they are about to make a complete statement

Illustrations:

I am sure the newly passed economic bill will favor us; **for example,** allowing foreign investors, releasing bonds to citizens in diaspora, investing in infrastructure and encouraging exportation of local products will return our economy back to the seat of glory.

I have told you before; **i.e.,** drinking and driving will truncate his life.

Where you do not have conjunctions words such as "and," a semicolon is good to be applied.

Incorrect   Let's meet at the bar I have good news for you.
                 Can you come to my office I have a job for you.

Correct   Let's meet at the bar; I have good news for you.
                 Can you come to my office; I have a job for you.

Quotation Marks ("")

To write intelligently in English language, quotation mark is a member of punctuation marks category you cannot do without. Whether you are writing formally or informally, you must use the quotation marks in a sentence, word or phrase. When you put quotation marks on a word, phrase or clause, in a sentence, such word, phrase or clause, becomes "quoted." What are the rules to follow in avoiding quotation marks errors in English grammar? Read on!

If you need to quote a question statement, ensure to put quotation marks after the question mark. Quotation marks, when used, always carry the larger power above other punctuation in a sentence.

Incorrect   "After doing that, what next"?He asked.

He said to her, "Do you think we can have a kiss"?

She said, "He said, are you finished with the homework"?

Correct   "After doing that, what next?" he asked.

He said to her, "Do you think we can have a kiss after the class?"

She said, "He said, are you finished with the homework?"

Punctuation marks like comma, ellipsis, and period used in sentences remain in the quotation marks. Irrespective of the number of other kinds of punctuation marks in a sentence, once you need to quote, you must quote the whole sentence.

Incorrect

"A real soldier, who is not afraid of death, should be loyal, and fight for his country"…

"I am going to be the best version of myself; a man of virtue, optimistic, careful and always looking to make use of every opportunity even when everything appears difficult".

Melisa said, "James said, 'Put my phone on silence'".

Correct

"A real soldier, who is not afraid of death, should be loyal, and fight for his country…"

"I am going to be the best version of myself; a man of virtue, optimistic, careful and always looking to make use of every opportunity even when everything appears difficult."

Melisa said, "James said, 'Put my phone on silence.'"

Apostrophe (')

For possessive words, use apostrophe.

Look at Abraham's curvy head.

That is the man's son.

Behind john is Dave's belt.

That back-pack is his sister's, not his.

For names ending with "-s," put apostrophe to show possession

Incorrect   In Jesus' name we pray.

Those materials are Mr. Rawlings'.

Lees's car is the best I've ever seen in my entire life.

Twenty miles from here, is my brother-in-laws' apartment.

Correct   In Jesus's name we pray.

Those materials are Mr. Rawlings's.

Lees's car is the best I've ever seen in my entire life.

Twenty miles from here, is my brother-in-law's apartment.

For word contraction, use apostrophe where the letter omitted is removed.

e.g.,

you are	you're
I am	I'm
They are	they're
He is	he's
Where is	where's
That is	that's
It is	it's

To use apostrophe for plural nouns to show possession, ensure the noun is pluralized first, then you should add apostrophe.

Incorrect

We are in the mens' world.

There is the womens' locker.

The actresses's costume is here.

That is the Johns's house.

Correct

We are in the men's world.

There is the women's locker.

The actresses' costume is here.

That is the Johns' residence.

Avoid forming plurals for numbers and capital letters using apostrophe

e.g.,

Incorrect

I was born in the **90's.**

She got married in the **1880's**

She's a good learner as she has learned the **ABC's** of common errors in English grammar.

Correct   I was born in the **90s.**

She got married in the **1880s**

She's a good learner as she has learned the **ABCs** of common errors in English grammar.

Avoid using apostrophe with possessive words like his, hers, theirs, etc.

Incorrect   Although he believed the grade was his**'s**, she had always known it's hers**'s**.

The idea behind the innovation was theirs**'s.**

Those cupcakes belong to your brother, not your**'s.**

Correct   Although he believed the grade was his, she had always known it's hers.

The idea behind the innovation was theirs.

Those cupcakes belong to your brother,

not yours.

Hyphens (-)

Hyphens are used to showcase compound words. These compound words may come as two, three or four words to refer to a single thing. Before studying the rules attached to learning how hyphen is used, look at the examples below:

> Eye-opening (meaning that an unexpected revelation is being revealed)
> Mother-in-law (the mother of your wife)
> Door-in-the-face (using big request as a means to get other smaller requests)
> Foot-in-the-door (the opposite of the Door-in-the-face)

Now, let's check out the rules you must not break in hyphenation.

The first rule in hyphenation is: *before you think of hyphenating two unfamiliar words, make sure you check them up in your dictionary.* This will enable you to be sure that you are not making a mistake. Most times, the major mistakes students make is that they use unfamiliar words and hyphenate them before taking time to find out. For example, "eyewitness" must never be hyphenated, but "eye–opener" exists in the dictionary hyphenated, and not joined together. This makes the rule valid that your dictionary must be your closest pal if you desire to be very good at hyphenating words.

Use hyphen when you have two or more adjectival words appearing before a noun and serving as a single meaning.

Illustrations

Before she met me, she only knew little that I am such a **handsome-looking** man.

It was a **record-breaking** experience in my family to be the first to meet Donald Trump.

Hyphenate when you have adverbs used as compound sentences in front of a noun.

Incorrect
A **well known** record about the indicted artist was banned last week.

The **long awaited** engagement took place last week.

Correct
A **well-known** record about the indicted artist was banned last week.

The **long-awaited** engagement took place

last week.

Ensure to hyphenate words that state fractions of numbers and compound numbers like twenty-one and so on.

e.g.,

Incorrect	To bake cake, you need **one fifth** of a tin of milk…
	I will be **twenty four** on July fourth.
Correct	To bake cake, you need **one-fifth** of a tin of milk…
	I will be twenty-four on July fourth.

Dash (–)

Dashes are interesting and rare punctuation marks in English grammar. The difference between a dash and hyphen is in the "length." A dash is typically longer than hyphen. And another outstanding difference is that; while a hyphen helps separate compound words, a dash is mostly used to complement an already existing sentence with another related sentence.

For example, *using a dash for open compound words*, you can have "a primary school – secondary debate competition."

You can use a dash to state time frame of an event.

e.g., the historic incident occurred during the years 1990 – 2030.

Also, use dash to elaborate more on your sentence only in a conversational style of writing.

e.g.,"…the Ruger 57 pistol has fantastic features of the 5.7 round such as flat shooting and soft clicking – enabling you to shoot multiple rounds at targeted positions."

Remember; consistency is the key to remembering the rules and how to avoid errors in punctuation marks. Keep studying and practicing – that's the way to expertise.

General MCQs on Punctuation marks: find the appropriate answer to the following.

1. She's at the ___ office.

>A. M.D.'s
>
>B. M.D.s

Answer: A

2. How many dots should a standard ellipsis have?

>A. 2
>
>B. 3
>
>C. 4

Answer: B

3. I love my ________.

>A. Wife daughter and son
>
>B. Wife, daughter, and son
>
>C. Wife, daughter and son

Answer: B

4. Will you kiss the bride?__

> A. Yes pastor I will.
>
> B. Yes, Pastor, I will.
>
> C. Yes, Pastor I will.

Answer: B

5. They met on the 3rd of ____ 2019.

> A. May
>
> B. May,
>
> C. ,May

Answer: B

6. He needed to travel ___ he phoned his wife.

> A. ,so,
>
> B. so,
>
> C. so

Answer: A

7. I wish to speak with you (_) Can we talk later?

> **A.** :
>
> **B.** ;
>
> C. ,

Answer: B

8. Come with the following materials (_) glue, crayon and pencils.

   A. :

   B. ;

   C. ,

Answer: A

9. ____________ He asked.

   A. "How do I go about this"?

   B. "How do I go about this?"

   C. How do I go about this?"

Answer: B

10. She shouted, ________

   A. "Go away from me."

   B. "Go away from me".

Answer: A

11. I really don't know _____ heart I might have broken in the past year.

   A. Whose

   B. Who's

   C. What's

Answer: A

12. ___ at the door?

      A. Whose

      B. Whos

      C. Who's

Answer: C

13. Do you know if the company is ____ or ______?

      A. Task oriented / employee oriented

      B. Task-oriented / employee-oriented

      C. Task – oriented / employee – oriented

Answer: B

14. We need to have __________ association this session.

      A. Parent-teacher

      B. Parent – teacher

      C. Parent teacher

Answer: B

SENTENCE STRUCTURE AND COMPOSITION

A sentence is a statement that makes a complete though. Sentence structure is composed of many parts with the subject and predicate being the foundation of every sentence structure. In this chapter, we will explore errors that can arise from the wrong usage of various parts of a sentence.

Present Tense

A present tense describes an event that is currently taking place or a state of being. For example, "I am glad" is a present tense. Present tenses are considered to be easy to master. However, people still make mistakes despite their simplicity. Here are some common mistakes that are often made with the use of present tense:

Don't forget to add "s" to the end of the 3rd person singular in the present simple.

Incorrect   Kid's health **depend** on eating enough

vegetables

Correct   Kid's health **depends** on eating enough vegetables

Don't use the present simple for actions that are happening at the moment instead of present continuous.

Incorrect   He **walks** so slowly

Correct   He is **walking** so slowly

Don't use "will" instead of the present simple to express a future action after words such as "whether, if, as soon as, before".

Incorrect   If the weather **will be** bad, we will not go to the mall

Correct   If the weather **is** bad, we will not go to the mall

Don't use the present continuous when talking about well-known facts instead of present simple

Incorrect   The earth **is revolving** around the sun

Correct   The earth **revolves** around the sun

Don't use the present continuous after words that express emotions.

Incorrect   Father **is loving** you to the moon and back

Correct   Father **loves** you to the moon and back

Use the present perfect when talking about something that was not completed until the moment of speaking.

Incorrect   I **am waiting** for you since 7 o'clock

Correct   I **have been waiting** for you since 7 o'clock

MCQs: choose the appropriate options from the statements below

Whatever _________ up comes down. (A. is going B. goes)

Answer: B

He _____ vibrantly and passionately. (A. speak B. speaks)

Answer: B

Past Tense

A past tense shows that an action occurred in the past. An

example of a past tense is "I ate rice last week". Below are common errors in the use of past tenses and how to use them appropriately:

Do not use the past continuous but past simple to talk about past habits.

Incorrect I **was walking** to church every day when I was young

Correct I **walked** to church every day when I was young

Don't use the continuous to emphasize completed events at a particular time in the past but past simple.

Incorrect I **was calling** his office at 5 o'clock yesterday evening

Correct I **called** his office at 5 o'clock yesterday evening

Do not use present perfect or past perfect but past simple when referring to a definite time in the past.

Incorrect I **have woken up** at 6 o'clock this morning

Correct I **woke up** at 6 o'clock this morning

Don't use the past simple but present perfect to refer to time up to now

Incorrect   I **didn't pay** my electricity bill yet

Correct   I **haven't paid** my electricity bill yet

Don't use the past continuous but the past simple to repeat main events.

Incorrect   She **was cycling** to Ben's house last night

Correct   She **cycled** to Ben's house last night

Don't use the past continuous in the same way as "used to" when talking about things that used to happen but no longer true.

Incorrect   We **were** playing games in the park in the summer

Correct   We **used to** play games in the park in the summer

MCQs: choose the appropriate options from the statements below

Ben _______ swept the room yet (A. didn't B. haven't)

Answer: B

David _____ to Trump's house yesterday (A. walked B. was walking)

Answer: A

Future Tense

A future tense in grammar is a verb that reflects that the event described by the verb will happen in the future. Future tense can be in the form of simple future tense, future continuous tense, future perfect tense, and future perfect continuous tense.

Example:

I will pay you a visit as soon as possible.

The most common future tense mistakes are depicted and corrected below:

Don't miss out on "is/am/are" when using the "going to" form.

Incorrect   I **going to** wash the clothes tomorrow

Correct   I **am going to** wash the clothes tomorrow

Don't miss out on "to" when you are using the "going to" form

Incorrect He is **going** eat that fruit again

Correct He is **going to** eat that fruit again

Don't add "to" when using "will"

Incorrect She **will to** be sorry

Correct She **will** be sorry

Don't use the "-ing" form of the verb instead of the base form with "will" or "going to".

Incorrect She **will winning** the match

Incorrect She is **going to winning** the match

Correct She **will win** the match

MCQs: choose the appropriate options from the statements below

He _________ angry (A. will be B. will to be)

Answer: A

She is _____ dance again (A. going B. going to)

Answer: B

1st Person

By taking note of the pronouns in a sentence, you will be able to know whether it s a first, second, or third grammatical person. Pronouns such as "I" and "my" depicts that a person is writing in first-person. First-person pronouns can also be in plural forms such as "we", "our", and "us".

Examples:

I am not oblivious to that fact.

We can stay at home if you allow **us**.

It can be tricky to write in first-person as it can be easy to make mistakes. Below are common mistakes associated with writing in first-person:

Don't end a sentence with "I"

Incorrect   Jackson talked with **I**

Correct   Jackson talked with **me**

Don't start a sentence with "me"

Incorrect   **Me** and Ben went to the market yesterday

Correct   Ben and **I** went to the market yesterday

Don't say "between you and I", say "between you and me"

Incorrect   Let's keep this **between you and I**

Correct   Let's keep this **between you and me**

MCQs: choose the appropriate options from the statements below

David and _______ will be coming to your house (A. I B. me)

Answer: A

The feud between you and ____ will never end (A. I B. me)

Answer: B

2nd Person

Just like their first-person counterparts, it can be tricky to use second-person pronouns too. The second-person refers to the audience of the speaker. Pronouns such as "you" and "your" depict the second-person. It is the context of the statement that decides whether it is a singular or plural form of second-person that is being used.

Examples:

You have to be careful.

Your dog is cute.

Here are some common errors people make when speaking or writing second-person pronouns:

Avoid shifting from second-person to first or third person in a sentence

Incorrect	We wanted to learn swimming from a coach but we found out that **you** can learn online
Correct	We wanted to learn swimming from a coach but we found out that **we** can learn online
Incorrect	If you are focused, **most people** will be able to achieve **their** dreams
Correct	If you are focused, **you** will be able to achieve **your** dreams

MCQs: choose the appropriate options from the statements below

If most people eat healthily, _______ will live longer (A. I B. they)

Answer: B

We will work hard because that is how ____ can become wealthy (A. we B. you)

Answer: A

Third Person

Third-person is a form of pronoun or verb that reflects that are talking about someone or something other than yourself or your direct audience. It distances the writer or speaker from the character it presents in a sentence.

Examples:

He is an exemplary leader.

They have a knack for producing good music.

Students and speakers of English language are susceptible

to using the third person in a wrong way. Below are some common errors and the appropriate usage:

Ensure you add "s" to the verb form when writing about the habit of a singular subject

Incorrect   He **become** annoyed when told to keep quiet

Correct   He **becomes** annoyed when told to keep quiet

Don't add "s" to the verb form writing about the habit of plural subjects

Incorrect   They **becomes** sad when told to keep quiet

Correct   They **become** sad when told to keep quiet

Third-person plural should take singular verb forms and vice versa

Incorrect   She **have** a car

Correct   She **has** a car

MCQs: choose the appropriate options from the statements below

Superman _________ his energy from the sun (A. derives B. derive)

Answer: A

Ben and John _____ the license to roam freely in this compound (A. has B. have)

Answer: B

Subject

In English Grammar, the subject refers to the part of a sentence that indicates what or who performed or performs an action. The subject is usually a noun. However, there are also subject pronouns. In declarative statements, subjects usually come after the verb.

Examples:

The lion roars.

My sister's bag looks nice.

Typical errors associated with the usage of subject include the following:

Don't use present continuous to express possession; use present simple tense

Incorrect   I **am having** four cars

Correct   I **have** four cars

Avoid using "do not" after subjects pronouns such as "he", "it", and "she"

Incorrect   She **do not** possess a mobile phone

Correct   She **does not** possess a mobile phone

When using "cope", don't add "up to it" to describe the coping ability of the subject

Incorrect   Jackson struggled to **cope up** with the pressure

Correct   Jackson struggled to **cope** with the pressure

When comparing two individuals, "than" should be

followed by "that"

Incorrect   The quantity of his rice is **higher than** yours

Correct   The quantity of his rice is **higher thanthat** of yours

MCQs: choose the appropriate options from the statements below

He ________ possess leadership qualities (A. do not B. does not)

Answer: B

Poor people _____ the tendency to blame others for their predicaments (A. has B. have)

Answer: B

Predicate

The predicate is the part of a clause or sentence that reveals the action of the subject. The predicate also tells us what the subject it. It is every other thing in a sentence that is not the subject.

Examples:

I **sing**.

He **was cooking** dinner when I came in.

There are many errors students and professionals make due to the wrong usage of predicates. Some of them are covered here:

When you start a statement with "once upon a time", you have to use past tense all through

Incorrect   Once upon a time, there **is** a dog named Elvis

Correct   Once upon a time, there **was** a dog named Elvis

"Did" should be followed by present tense

Incorrect   Philips did not **trained** with the first team yesterday

Correct   Philips did not **train** with the first team yesterday

Pronouns must agree with the nouns they are replacing

Incorrect   Bob and **her** friend were not around when we go there

Correct   Bob and **his** friend were not around when we go there

MCQs: choose the appropriate options from the statements below

Once upon a time, a village chief _________ a magic box (A. was given B. is given)

Answer: A

Fernandez and Ricardo did not _____ until our arrival (A. leave B. left)

Answer: B

Direct Objects

In English grammar, direct objects follow intransitive verbs. Direct objects can be a noun, pronoun, phrase or verb. They identify who or what receives the action of a transitive verb in a sentence or clause. The action of the subject is felt by the direct object. For example, in the statement, "Craig baked a cake", the direct object is "a cake". Here are some common errors writers and speakers of English language commit when using direct objects:

Don't add "s" to "furniture"

Incorrect	My father bought some **furnitures** yesterday
Correct	My father bought some **furniture** yesterday

Don't add "s" to "information"

Incorrect	Have you got any **informations** on the where about of Sala?
Correct	Have you got any **information** on the where about of Sala?

Don't add "s" to "luggage"

Incorrect	When will you pack your **luggages**?
Correct	When will you pack your **luggage**?

Don't add "s" to the noun after "any"

Incorrect	Is there any **breads** at home?
Correct	Is there any **bread** at home?

Avoid using "these" before "news"

Incorrect	She told me **these** news this morning.

Correct   She told me **this** news this morning.

Don't add "s" to expressions like "the blind", "the poor", the dead" or "the unemployed".

Incorrect   It is high time the American Government started paying attention to **the poors**

Correct   It is high time the American Government started paying attention to **the poor**

MCQs: choose the appropriate options from the statements below

I have some vital _______ for you as regards the case. (A. information B. informations)

Answer: A

The ____ I saw at the King's palace were nothing other than amazing! (A. furnitures B. furniture)

Answer: A

Indirect Objects

Indirect objects receive the action of the subject after the action has first affected the direct object. They are not the direct recipients of the action but they are affected too. It is important to note that it is not all sentences that have a direct object that have indirect objects. For instance, in the sentence, "I threw the ball but Andrew got it", "Andrew" is an indirect object. Below are some common errors associated with indirect objects:

Put the indirect object at the end of the sentence when using "to"

Incorrect   She gave **to** John her pencil.

Correct   She gave her pencil **to** John.

You cannot have an indirect object for intransitive verbs

Incorrect   Henry is snoring **drugs** heavily

Correct   Henry is **snoring** heavily

MCQs: choose the appropriate options from the statements below

Please send _________ . (A. to me the report B. the report to me)

Answer: B

Jonathan _____ on the ice (A. skidded B. skidded the ball)

Answer: A

Clauses

A clause refers to a group of words that has both a subject and a predicate. However, clause cannot always be regarded as a full grammatical sentence. A clause can either be dependent or independent. An independent clause can stand alone and contains both a predicate and a subject. For example, "We visited Luxemburg last October" is an independent clause.

A dependent clause is also called a subordinate clause. It contains a subject and predicate but cannot stand alone as a sentence. In the sentence, "**Even though he made $400 million**, he remains grounded", the highlighted part is the dependent clause. Below are some common errors associated with clauses:

A defining subordinate clause should be introduced with "that" not "which".

Incorrect   The river **which** flows through Lisbon is
                  murky

Correct   The river **that** flows through Lisbon is
                 murky

A non-defining subordinate clause should be introduced
with "which" not "that" while being separated with two
commas.

Incorrect   The Nigerian river Benue, **that** flows
                 through Niger, is murky and turbid

Correct   The Nigerian river Benue, **which** flows
                 through Niger, is murky and turbid

A defining subordinate clause should be introduced with
"who" not "whose".

Incorrect   The American military officer **whose**
                 defeated the Italians became the President

Correct   The American military officer **who**
                 defeated the Italians became the President

A non-defining subordinate clause should be introduced
with "whose" not "who" while being separated with two
commas.

Incorrect   The King of England, **who** kingship was
                 the reward for his heroics, was an unusual

man

Correct   The King of England, **whose** kingship was the reward for his heroics, was an unusual man

MCQs: choose the appropriate options from the statements below

The Duke of Wellington, _________ peerage was the reward for his patriotism, was a great man. (A. who B. whose)

Answer: B

The teacher _____ came yesterday is my friend. (A. that B. which)

Answer: A

Run Ons

A run-on sentence is a common error as a result of merging two sentences together without the right punctuation. The comma splice or comma fault is the most common run-out sentence. A comma splice occurs when a comma is used to separate two sentences in an appropriate manner.

Examples:

Craig is a brilliant soccer player, he dances in an amazing way.

My mum is such a good cook; she gets angry at the slightest provocation.

To avoid these kinds of errors, do the following:

Use a semicolon

Incorrect   Racism is not exclusive to any **culture;** it is a demon we all have to resist.

Correct   Racism is not exclusive to any **culture,** it is a demon we all have to resist

Use three dots (ellipsis)

Incorrect   I could not have been acting **funny,** I am a poor comedian

Correct   Racism I could not have been acting **funny...** I am a poor comedian

Use a colon

Incorrect   I have a **confession,** I don't like making confessions!

Correct   I have a **confession:** I don't like making confessions!

MCQs: choose the appropriate options from the statements below

I don't care about your welfare________ it is all you care about (A. , B. ;)

Answer: B

The teacher ____ came yesterday is my friend. (A. that B. which)

Answer: A

Subordinators

Subordinators are not relative or subordinate clauses; they introduce them and join them to a main clause. A subordinator can be a relative noun that introduces an adjective clause, adverb clause, or noun clause in a sentence.

Examples:

Whoever claimed **that the sun revolves around the earth** was dead wrong.

My mother enjoyed **where my father selected** for their honeymoon.

Common errors related to subordinators are as follows:

Thinking that a dependent clause makes a complete sentence

Incorrect	Because we love Kobe Brant
Correct	**We are here** because we love Kobe Bryant

Use a comma when you start a sentence with a subordinator

Incorrect	Because we love Kobe **Brant we** are here
Correct	Because we love Kobe **Brant, we** are here

The subordinator should come before a verb

Incorrect   I went to the market after, I stopped at the bank

Correct   After I went to the market after, I stopped at the bank

MCQs: choose the appropriate options from the statements below

Which of these two statements are correct? (A. She sold the food before, she persuaded the buyer B. Before she sold the food, she persuaded the buyer)

Answer: B

Due to _____ she could not make it. (A. technical reasons, B. technical reasons)

Answer: A

Phrases

A phrase is a group of words used within a sentence as a unit to express a concept. Types of phrases include noun, gerund, appositive, infinitive, absolute, prepositional, participial, and verb.

Examples:

Sunday became **a cool, wet afternoon**

She **might enjoy a massage**

Do you know your phrases? Let's see:

It is "one and the same" and not "one in the same"

Incorrect   The two balls are **one in the same**

Correct   The two balls are **one and the same**

It is "each one worse than the last" and not "each one worse than the next"

Incorrect   The disasters kept coming, **each one worse than the next**

Correct   The disasters kept coming, **each one worse than the last**

It is "by accident" and not "on accident"

Incorrect   The truck crushed the puppy **on** accident

Correct   The truck crushed the puppy **by** accident

MCQs: choose the appropriate options from the statements below

Dan slapped him to _____ revenge on him (A. exact B. extract)

Answer: A

I am giving you _____ to make your choice. (A. leadway B. leeway)

Answer: B

Noun/Verb Phrases

A noun phrase is also referred to a nominal phrase. These phrases have a noun as their head. They are very common and arguably the most common of all the types of phrase.

Examples:

Those apparels are very expensive

I possess **a lot of money.**

A Verb phrase, on the other hand, is a part of a sentence structure that contains both the verb as well as an indirect or direct object. Verb phrases are upgrades on verbs because they contain both the verb as well as the complement.

Examples:

Mike **was walking** quickly to the market.

Our maid **is fixing** us a dinner.

Common errors people make when they use noun and verb phrases are displayed below:

Don't use a past participle instead of a continuous tense to express an ongoing action

Incorrect   The teacher **is written** a report

Correct   The teacher **is writing** a report

Never forget to add an "e" in the "-ed" form of regular verbs

Incorrect   Kate and Vanessa **joind** the team last year

Correct   Kate and Vanessa **joined** the team last year

The plural form of "scenery" is not "sceneries"

Incorrect   The **sceneries** here **are** not pleasant

Correct   The **scenery** here **are** not pleasant

Don't add "brother" to "cousin"

Incorrect   Bob is my **cousin brother**

Correct   Bob is my **cousin**

MCQs: choose the appropriate options from the statements below

One of my _____ will be coming for the party. (A. friends B. friend)

Answer: A

I am learning a new _____. (A. poetry B. poem)

Answer: B

Prepositional/Absolute

Prepositional phrases act as indirect objects in a sentence. Prepositions are used to specify why, how, where, and when. Hence, a prepositional phrase has a preposition and its object. A prepositional phrase can be a group of words or a single word expressing an idea.

Examples:

Yesterday was the first day **of the month**.

Last week, we met **in the auditorium.**

Absolute phrases tell more about a circumstance or situation in the main clause of a sentence. They are also known as nominative absolute because they contain a noun and its modifiers. They can be placed in the beginning, middle, or end of a sentence.

Examples

The night beginning to turn cold, we made fire to keep us warm.

The birds circled high above us, **their tiny frames sleek and brown against the blue sky.**

Common errors both students and professional alike make when using absolutes and prepositional phrases are explored below:

When describing a request, "for" should follow "ask"

Incorrect	She **asked** a drink
Correct	She **asked for** a drink

Don't add "with" to "met or meet"

Incorrect	I **met with** your mum last month at a party
Correct	I **met** your mum last month at a party

"Insist" should be followed by "on" and not "on"

Incorrect	My father insisted **to** seeing my report sheet
Correct	My father insisted **on** seeing my report sheet

Don't fail to separate the absolute phrase with a comma

Incorrect   **Weather permitting** we shall meet

tomorrow

Correct   **Weather permitting,** we shall meet

tomorrow

MCQs: choose the appropriate options from the statements below

The sun having ____, we set out on our journey. (A. rose B. risen)

Answer: B

He will insist ____ speaking with you. (A. on B. to)

Answer: A

Appositives

Appositives are nouns or pronouns that identify or rename another noun or pronoun in some certain ways. A typical appositive phrase consists of an appositive and its modifiers. An appositive phrase can either be restrictive (essential) or nonrestrictive (nonessential).

Examples

Author **Oscar Wilde** wrote several books over the course of his career.

Williams Shakespeare novel, **Macbeth**, remains one of the best art works ever.

While writing and speaking, the following error is often committed when using appositives:

Separate with commas where and when necessary

Incorrect   Bruno **Fernandes a former Sporting Lisbon player** has just signed for Manchester United

Correct   Bruno **Fernandes, a former Sporting Lisbon player,** has just signed for Manchester United

MCQs: Select the underlined word or phrase that needs to be changed to make the sentence accurate

Merlin, the wizard of Oz, has summoned every wizard in the world to a meeting at Old Trafford. (A. the wizard of Oz, B. No error C. wizard in the world)

Answer: B

<u>The dogs, who</u> were <u>basset hounds were</u> never in doubt to win the one-sided race. (A. The dogs, who B. basset hounds were)

Answer: B

Introductions

An introduction is the beginning section of a book or article. It is the first few paragraphs that states out the goals of the writing and what readers can expect as they read on. Check the introductory part of this book for further reference on what an introduction looks like. It does not necessarily have to be much. It is a brief summary or explanation of a document.

A good introduction will achieve the following:

- It will answer the question of "why should I read this?"
- It engages the audience
- It gives the readers a preview of the material

There is a good and bad way to write an introduction. When writing an introduction, you should avoid the following things:

- **Wasting words**: Don't just write to fill a blank space. You should be deliberate and intentional with every sentence.

- **Using long sentences**: It becomes difficult and boring when you have close to 40 to 50 words in a sentence. It is pardonable in an academic writing but not good for articles or blog posts.

- **Making promises you cannot fulfill:** You should not tell your readers that they will find what is not obtainable in the article in your introduction. Encourage your audience to read on without being dishonest.

- **Explaining concepts you will still explain later in the book or article:** It becomes monotonous and repetitive when you explain a concept you will still explain later in the book in the introductory part.

Note: You can work on the body of the article or book first before writing the introduction. This is not a rule you have to follow. However, it will help you to write a better introduction. You already have the content of the book. Hence, you will be able to tell the readers what to expect with a greater level of precision and accuracy.

MCQs: choose the appropriate options from the statements below

A good paragraph is____ (A. Precise and concise B. unnecessarily detailed)

Answer: A

Several long sentences in a paragraph are a feature of ____. (A. a good introduction B. a bad introduction)

Answer: B

Body Paragraphs

A body paragraph is a group or collection of related sentences about a particular idea. The writer achieves his or her objectives with the body paragraphs as stated out in the introduction. Essays and articles contain several body paragraphs. Hence, the main errors committed as regards body paragraphs apart from grammatical errors have to do with organization. It is vital that a writer is able to arrange his or her thoughts in such a way that he or she will be able to drive home his or her points.

Common Mistakes In Writing A Paragraph

Below are 5 common mistakes that are made in writing paragraphs:

- **Absence of a topic sentence**: A good paragraph must have a topic sentence. The topic sentence carries the main idea you are trying to convey to your readers. Subsequent sentences in the paragraph are meant to support the topic sentence.

- **Too long paragraphs:** When a paragraph is too long, it frustrates readers. You should never forget that there are people that will read what you are writing. Hence, avoid writing more than 8 sentences in a paragraph.

- **Too short paragraphs:** Some students are fond of writing two to three sentences in a paragraph. A paragraph should be detailed and concise about the central idea you are passing across.

- **Multiple ideas:** A paragraph should only explain a particular line of thought or idea. You should avoid clamping several ideas into one paragraph.

- **Poor structure:** Poor structure in writing a paragraph can be related to the arrangement or focus of the paragraphs. Every paragraph should have a focus. It is better to start with a topic sentence first before writing the subordinate sentences.

MCQs: choose the appropriate options from the statements below

A good paragraph should start with _____ (A. a topic sentence B. an explanation)

Answer: A

Multiple ideas in a body paragraph should be _____. (A. embraced B. avoided)

Answer: B

Conclusions

A conclusion is the closing part of a document or write-up. When you write an article, paper, or book, the conclusion is the part where you sum up your arguments and points. It is a summary of everything you have been trying to discuss and put across to your audience. You have to think about the main points of the book to be able to write a good conclusion.

Common Errors You Should Avoid When Writing A Conclusion

You should avoid the following mistakes when writing a conclusion:

- **Introducing new information:** Your conclusion should not contain any information that you have not mentioned previously.

- **Stuffing too much information into a paragraph:** In case of a book or an academic writing, you may have a reasonable number of things you want to mention in the introduction. However, you have to avoid stuffing a lot of information in a paragraph. Break things up to make it easier and organized to read.

- **Not including a topic sentence:** The rule of topic sentence for a body paragraph also applies to a conclusion. The paragraphs of your conclusion should have a topic sentence in the first or second statement.
- **Lack of cohesion:** Your words and sentences should transition smoothly. Avoid writing dissimilar sentences together in a paragraph to make your writing cohesive and coherent.

MCQs: choose the appropriate options from the statements below

When writing a conclusion, you should _____ (A. introduce a new concept B. reiterate previous ideas)

Answer: B

A good conclusion should _____. (A. lack cohesion B. be summative)

Answer: B

Thesis

A thesis is also called a dissertation. It is a document that contains your research and findings that you submit to show that you are qualified to possess a professional certification or academic degree. A good thesis contains what you intend to argue and how you intend to argue it. A thesis statement often appears at the latter part of the introductory paragraph of the paper. It offers the readers a concise summary of the claim of a research paper.

Common Errors In Thesis Statement

The following mistakes in thesis statement can embarrass you:

Fragmented statement: A thesis must make a complete thought. You cannot have fragmented statements as a thesis statement. For example:

Incorrect   The food in the UK is unhealthy and expensive; so we should all consider not eating them again.

Correct   Due to the prevalence of obesity in the UK, lawmakers should look into creating a plan to reduce the price of healthier foods to help everyone to be able to afford high-quality foods.

Wordiness: Your thesis statement should not be too wordy. You will confuse your readers when you thesis statement is too long. Make it as short, detailed, and precise as possible.

Incorrect — Most athletes, such as those who play for organizations like the NCAA or colleges, do not earn enough money, which is terrible because they deserve to earn more for their hard work due to the fact that colleges take advantage of the sports these athletes pay by earning profits.

Correct — NCAA athletes should be given payment that is commensurate to their efforts because they are generating revenue for universities by putting their body and health on the line.

Too obvious or basic: It is expected that your writing should mature as you move through school. Hence, an obvious or basis thesis statement is not accepted.

Incorrect — In this paper, I will be discussing the

importance of getting enough sleep every day.

Correct Getting adequate sleep is good for your health as it helps your body recover quickly and have enough energy required for optimal performance in your daily tasks.

Lack of purpose: Your thesis statement should be addressing a particular thing. It should not just be a random cluster of words.

Incorrect As far as I am concerned, these blue socks are the prettiest ones in the drawer.

Correct Students should be given the liberty to express themselves as unique individuals by selecting any type of socks and shoes they want to wear to school.

MCQs: choose the appropriate options from the statements below

An excellent thesis statement should be _____ (A. basic and obvious B. purposeful and concise)

Answer: B

A wordy thesis statement is _____. (A. confusing B. the best)

Answer: A

SPELLING AND FORMATTING

Words are the foundation of English grammar. Once you spell a word wrongly, you will either create a new word and alter the meaning of the word or create a meaningless word. Therefore, it is imperative that you pay attention to the spelling of words. You have to spell words correctly consistently as a good writer of English language. In this chapter, we will explore common spelling errors as well as the wrong usage of some other important components of English grammar.

Common Spelling Mistakes

It is important that you spell words correctly to pass the right message. Spelling errors lead to an embarrassing mutation of words. Hence, you have to be at the top of your game all the time. A list of common spelling mistakes will be endless. Below are some most common spelling mistakes you need to avoid:

Incorrect   acceptible

Correct   acceptable

Incorrect   absense, absance

Correct   absence

Incorrect   accomodate

Correct   accommodate

Incorrect   acknowlege, aknowledge

Correct   acknowledge

Incorrect   acquaintence, aquaintance

Correct   acquaintance

Incorrect   aquire

Correct   acquire

Incorrect   adultary

Correct   adultery

Incorrect   adress

Correct   address

Incorrect   accidentaly

Correct   accidentally

Incorrect   adviseable, advizable

Correct   advisable

Incorrect   aquit

Correct   acquit

Incorrect   agression

Correct   aggression

Incorrect   allegaince

Correct   allegiance

Incorrect   allmost

Correct   almost

Incorrect   amatuer

Correct   amateur

Incorrect   anualy

Correct   annually

Incorrect   aparent, aparent

Correct   apparent

Incorrect   awfull

Correct   awful

Incorrect   begining

Correct   beginning

Incorrect   buisness

Correct   business

Incorrect   colum

Correct   column

Incorrect   cauhgt, caugt

Correct   caught

Incorrect	congradulate
Correct	congratulate
Incorrect	concencus
Correct	consensus
Incorrect	cooly
Correct	coolly
Incorrect	contraversy
Correct	controversy
Incorrect	dilema
Correct	dilemma
Incorrect	embarass
Correct	embarrass
Incorrect	facinating
Correct	fascinating
Incorrect	immitate

Correct   imitate

Incorrect   innoculate

Correct   inoculate

Incorrect   writting

Correct   writing

Incorrect   visious

Correct   vicious

MCQs: choose the appropriate options from the statements below

It is ____ to know that you will be coming around. (A. facinating B. fascinating C. fasinating)

Answer: B

I will not be able to ____ you in my house. (A. accommodate B. acomodate C. accomodate)

Answer: A

This sanitary pad is no longer ____. (A. usable B. usible C. ucible)

Answer: A

The _____ of the President is no longer acceptable to the citizens of the nation. (A. tyranny B. tyrany C. tiranny)

Answer: A

Vowels

In the above examples, I deliberately did not include common spelling errors that have to do with the misplacement or elimination of vowels. There are some common mistakes people make when writing words some words due to either a removal or misplacement of vowels. Such mistakes are seen below:

Incorrect   upholstry

Correct   upholstery

Incorrect   tomatos

Correct   tomatoes

Incorrect   then

Correct   than

Incorrect   speache, speeche

Correct   speech

Incorrect   similer

Correct   similar

Incorrect   sargent

Correct   sergeant

Incorrect   seperate

Correct   separate

Incorrect   secretery, secratary

Correct   secretary

Incorrect   rime

Correct   rhyme

Incorrect   restarant, restaraunt

Correct   restaurant

Incorrect   religous, religius

Correct	religious
Incorrect	realy
Correct	really
Incorrect	readible
Correct	readable
Incorrect	quarentine
Correct	quarantine
Incorrect	prufe
Correct	proof
Incorrect	professer
Correct	professor
Incorrect	parliment
Correct	parliament

MCQs: choose the appropriate options from the statements below

I must confess that some of your claims are _____. (A. outrageous B. outragous C. outrageos)

Answer: A

My father has the _____ that Mr. Ben is a philanderer. (A. prufe B. proof C. prove)

Answer: B

There is a need for a thorough _____ of foreigners due to the outbreak of the coronary. (A. quarantine B. quaranteine C. quarentine)

Answer: A

I am an _____; I am not_____. (A. atheist, religious B. athiest, religious C. athiest, religous)

Answer: A

"I Before E"

There are spelling errors that are peculiar to placing "I" before "e" and vice versa. These errors are also numerous. Below are some common examples:

Incorrect   percieve

Correct   perceive

Incorrect   acheive

Correct   achieve

Incorrect   athiest

Correct   atheist

Incorrect   beleive

Correct   believe

Incorrect   cheif

Correct   chief

Incorrect   decieve

Correct   deceive

Incorrect   foriegn

Correct   foreign

Incorrect   freind

Correct   friend

Incorrect   heirarchy

Correct   hierarchy

Incorrect   hygine, hygeine

Correct   hygiene

Incorrect   liesure

Correct   leisure

Incorrect   neice

Correct   niece

Incorrect   niegbour

Correct   neighbor

Incorrect   recieve

Correct   receive

MCQs: choose the appropriate options from the statements below

My _____ and I _____ a gift from my uncle. (A. niece, received B. niece, recieved C. neice, received)

Answer: A

I need to read a book to improve my English during my _____ time. (A. liesure B. leisure C. lecture)

Answer: B

The _____ of leadership in my country does not permit _____ to rule. (A. hierarchy, foreigners B. heirarchy, forigners C. hierarchy, foriegners)

Answer: A

Suffixes

Suffixes are a group of letters that are added to the ending part of words to alter their meaning or function. A suffix can also be just a letter. Suffices alter the grammatical function of the root word.

Examples

The highlighted letters below are examples of suffixes

Fond**est**

Art**ist**

Read**er**

Read**able**

Tas**ty**

Common Suffix Errors

There are mistakes people make when spelling words by getting the suffix wrong. Below are some common examples:

Incorrect   faithfull

Correct   faithful

Incorrect   accidentaly

Correct   accidently, accidentally

Incorrect   bellweather

Correct   bellwether

Incorrect   dumbell

Correct   dumbbell

Incorrect   drunkeness

Correct   drunkenness

Incorrect   equiptment

Correct   equipment

Incorrect   gratefull, greatful

Correct   grateful

Incorrect   mispell, misspel

Correct   misspell

Incorrect   skillfull

Correct   skilful

Incorrect   successfull

Correct   successful

MCQs: choose the appropriate options from the statements below

Donald trump says he is _____ to the good people of America for their indefatigable support. (A. grateful B. greatfull C. greatfool)

Answer: A

Stamford Bridge is a word-class stadium with state-of-the-art _____ and facilities. (A. equiptment B. equipment C. eqiupment)

Answer: B

_____ is fast becoming a prevalent social ill that has to be tackled quickly by the government of America. (A. drunkenness B. drunkeness C. drunkeeness)

Answer: A

Infixes

Infixes are word elements that can be added within the base form of a word to create a new word or alter the meaning the base word. Unlike prefixes or suffixes, infixes are not added to the beginning or end of the base form of a word. It is important to note that infixes are rarely used in formal writings.

Examples:

The infixes are highlighted in the words below:

Halle**bloody**lujah

Edu**ma**cation

sophisti**ma**cated

Common Mistakes When Writing Infixes

Unlike prefixes and suffixes, infixes are very rare. However, there are spelling mistakes people make when writing them. Here are some of them:

The plural form of "cupful" is not "cupfuls" but "cupsful"

Incorrect   cupfuls

Correct   cupsful

The plural form of "passerby" is not "passerbies" but "passersby"

Incorrect   passerbies

Correct   passersby

The plural form of "spoonful" is not "spoonfuls" but "spoonsful"

Incorrect   spoonfuls

Correct   spoonfuls

MCQs: choose the appropriate options from the statements below

An infix is an affix that can be inserted to the beginning or end of the base from of a word. (A. True B. false C. I don't care)

Answer: B

During the encounter between the cops and MS-13 gang at Los Angeles, innocent _____ were not spared by the deadly gang. (A. passerbies B. passersby C. passers by)

Answer: B

Prefixes

Prefixes are syllables or group of syllables that are added to the beginning of a word that alters the meaning or grammatical function of that word. With prefixes, it is possible to create different words that can be easily understood by writers and speakers everywhere.

Examples

The prefixes are highlighted in the examples below:

Disbelieve

Reevaluate

Deactivate

Illegal

Impermeable

Common Errors In Wring And Using Prefixes

Errors in adding prefixes often lead to creating words that does not exist. Below are some common errors people make when writing or using infixes

It should be "incorrect" and not "miscorrect" or "discorrect"

Incorrect	**mis**correct
Incorrect	**dis**correct
Correct	**in**correct

It should be "terror or counterterrorism" and not "noerror" or "counterterror"

Incorrect	**no**error
Incorrect	**counter**terror
Correct	**t**error, counterterrorism

It should be "discontented" and not "uncontented"

Incorrect	**un**contented
Correct	**dis**contented

MCQs: choose the appropriate options from the statements below

My failure to comply with the new policy was not out of defiance but because I was _____ of it. (A. misaware B. unaware C. disaware)

Answer: B

Today's protest is a product of _____ due to the way the workers were being treated by the manager recently. (A. uncontentment B. discontented C. discontentment)

Answer: C

Contradictions

A contradiction is as simple as your mum telling you two years ago that you were born in 1980 only for her to show up today to say that your birth date is 1981. The two statements are **contradicting.** In English grammar, a contradiction is a statement that does not make sense because some part of it suggests the opposite of the others.

Example

Larry is such an honest thief; he only steals cows.

The above statement is a contradiction because the fact that Larry is a thief means that there is nothing honest about him. Besides, stealing only cows does not make anyone honest!

Contradictions You Need To Watch Out For

English grammar has express rules. However, some of the rules have exceptions that lead to contradictions. Below are some rules in English grammar with contradictions:

I before E

English students are often told to put "I" before "e" when spelling except after "c". The following words follow that rule:

- Believe
- Brief
- Receive

Note: "e" came before "I" in "receive" because it was after the letter "c".

However, there are contradictions to this rule with words such as:

- Protein
- Heirloom
- Leisure
- Weird

Therefore, your spelling guide is your best bet to ensure that you are not running afoul of spelling words correctly.

Starting A Statement With" Because"

English students are also often told that because should not start a statement because it is a subordinate conjunction. It is often said that it needs a clause before it can relate to the one after. However, you can reverse the position of the clause and you will still be fine.

For example:

We did not visit the cinema yesterday because we were grounded.

Because we were grounded, we did not visit the cinema yesterday.

MCQs: choose the appropriate options from the statements below

It felt so _____ to be sharing the same stage with my idol. (A. wird B. weird C. wierd)

Answer: B

The new _____ teacher is just too hostile. (A. sceince B. sciene C. science)

Answer: C

Writing/Saying Dates

Dates specify the specific, day, month, and year that an event took place. Dates are vital because they serve historical and reference purposes. There are rules that guides the way dates are to be written in English. Below are some wrong ways people write dates and the appropriate way to go about them:

You should always write years in numerals except in the beginning of a sentence

Incorrect   The year **nineteen ninety-four** was indeed a memorable year for football lovers

Correct   The year **1994** was indeed a memorable year for football lovers

Correct   **Nineteen ninety-four** was indeed a memorable year for football lovers

Use cardinal numbers (one, two, three) and not ordinal numbers (first, second, third) when referring to a specific date in the month-day date format

Incorrect   Benjamin Burton was born on **May 13th**

Correct   Benjamin Burton was born on **May 13**

When using the month-day-year format, place commas after the day and the year

Incorrect   On October **1st, 1960** King Joe was born

Correct   On October **1st, 1960,** King Joe was born

Correct   On October 1, 1960, King Joe was born

Alternatively, don't use commas at all when using the day-month-year format

Incorrect   On 12 **October,** 1960 King Joe was born

Correct   On 12 **October** 1960 King Joe was born

You can use an ordinal number when you are referring to a specific say of the month without mentioning the year

Incorrect   Benjamin Burton was born **on the 13 of May**

Correct   Benjamin Burton was born **on the 13th of May**

Correct   Benjamin Burton was born **on the thirteenth**

Correct punctuation when writing days of the week

Incorrect   **Saturday May 7** is my last day of work

Correct   Saturday, May 7, is my last day of work

Avoid apostrophes when writing centuries

Incorrect   **In the 1800's,** men were more literate than in modern times

Correct   **In the 1800s,** men were more literate than in modern times

MCQs: choose the appropriate options from the statements below

The Titanic sank on _____. (A. 13 December 1914 B. 13 December, 1914 C. 13th December, 1914)

Answer: A

Women in the _____ were more courteous than today. (A. 1970s B. 1970's C. 1970s')

Answer: A

Numbers

It is always better to write out numbers 0 to one hundred in nontechnical writings. Generally, it is preferable to write out numbers under ten. However, you have to be consistent. Below are common errors you need to avoid when writing numbers in a sentence:

Write numbers below 101 fully

Incorrect   Ben said there are **40** reasons she likes rice and not twenty

Correct   Ben said there are **forty** reasons she likes

                 rice and not twenty

Write numbers above 101 numerically

Incorrect   In 2010, there were seventy-eight

                 thousand, nine hundred and thirty-nine

                 people living in Rio de Janeiro

Correct   In 2010, there were **78,939** people living

                 in Rio de Janeiro

It is "ninety" and not "ninty"

Incorrect   Ben said there are **ninty** reasons she likes

                 rice and not twenty

Correct   Ben said there are **ninety** reasons she likes

                 rice and not twenty

It is "forty" and not "fourty"

Incorrect   Ben said there are **fourty** reasons she likes

                 rice and not twenty

Correct   Ben said there are **forty** reasons she likes rice and not twenty

Always spell out a word that is starting a sentence

Incorrect **127** boys showed interest in the show

Correct **One hundred and twenty seven** boys showed interest in the show

Spell out round figures even when they are more than 101

Incorrect There were **5000** people in attendance during the show

Correct There were **five thousand** people in attendance during the show

MCQs: choose the appropriate options from the statements below

My mum gave me _____ mangoes before I left home. (A. ten B. 10)

Answer: A

I could not control my tears when I found out that _____ out of the _____ are dead. (A. 14, 403 B. fourteen C. 403)

Answer: B

Times And Clocks

It is inevitable to express time when writing once in a while. There are guidelines regarding how to show time when writing in English language. However, some people flout these rules either due to ignorance or negligence. Below are simple rules that will help you avoid making mistakes when telling the time in a written form:

Write times in numerical form except for midnight and noon

Incorrect   The match will take place from **eight a.m. to ten p.m.**

Correct   The match will take place from **8 a.m. to 10 p.m.**

Correct   The match will take place from **8 a.m. to noon**

Don't write "12" after writing "noon" or midnight

Incorrect   The workshop will begin by **12 noon**

Incorrect   The workshop will end by **12 midnight**

Correct   The workshop will begin by **noon**

Correct   The workshop will end by **midnight**

The lower case "a.m." and "p.m." should have periods

Incorrect   The workshop will end by **5 am**

Correct   The workshop will end by 5 a.m.

Don't use dash with days of the week

Incorrect   The workshop be from **8-11 a.m.** on Mondays to Thursday every month

Correct   The workshop be from **8 a.m. until 11 a.m.** on Mondays to Thursday every month

MCQs: choose the appropriate options from the statements below

My favorite TV show begins by _____ today (A. 10 p.m. B. Ten p.m.)

Answer: A

I have to wake up by _____ to read. (A. 12 midnight B. midnight)

Answer: B

ADVANCED WRITING MISTAKES

Whatever is worth doing at all should be done with the whole of your strength. It is good to be able to speak Basic English language for your daily needs. However, there is no reason why you should not aim at becoming an excellent writer and speaker of the language. It is important to note that you don't have to have a degree in English language to be able to speak fluently or write excellently in English. All you need is the drive to learn and acquire grammatical and writing skills.

In this last chapter, will explore advanced mistakes that even professional writers make when writing. The beautiful thing about knowing what not to do is that it will enable you to know what to do. Hence, knowing these mistakes will not only help you avoid them but write standard articles. If you have a dream to be an author or writer, this chapter is very critical for you. It is one thing to be able to spot spelling errors; it is another thing to spot issues that has to do with grammatical constructions.

General Advanced Writing Mistakes

Below are some general advanced writing mistakes you need to avoid to move from a mediocre to an excellent writer:

Not Defining The Goal Of Your Writing

The first thing you need to ask yourself when you want to write is why you are writing. The purpose of the writing will determine the tone of the writing. If you are writing an academic article, you know that you have to be formal all through. You cannot make random and careless statements in academic writings. You will have to get enough sources for the article before you start writing. Every claim in academic writing will have to be backed up by relevant studies. For example:

Incorrect   We all know that students of Harvard
                 University are better than students of Yale
                 when it comes to academic performance.

Correct   According to Steve and Maloney (2012), the academic performance of Harvard University students are better than that of students of Yale in the last five years.

For blog posts, you can be a little bit relaxed. It is required of you to add relevant studies to increase the veracity of your claims. However, it is not as stringent as when you are writing an academic paper. Hence, you need to be able to discern whether you are writing to entertain or to present facts for educational purposes.

The Right Content For The Wrong Audience And Vice Versa

It is not good enough to know the reason for your writing; you have to also know your audience. If your audiences are young people seeking fun, you have to write in such a way that will tickle their fancy. You will have to deliberately write to pique their interest. If your audiences are people in the academic setting, you will have to be very careful to present facts in a logical manner. They will scrutinize your arrangement of points and how you arrived at your conclusion.

In the same way, if you are writing an article that will be

read by kids, you have to make it as simple as possible. You will have to be deliberate about writing short, simple sentences that they can understand. You will have to use illustrations and bullet points to aid their comprehension. For example:

Incorrect	Snails are aquatic and terrestrial animals that hibernate during winter due to their ineptitude to withstand vociferous conditions.
Correct	Snails are animals that can live on both water and land. They go into hiding during winter to be able to survive harsh weather conditions

Fluff

Fluff in writing is unnecessary words that are redundant. They are often added just to fill up blank pages. Fluffs show that the writer is bereft of ideas. It is easy to detect fluffs because of their tendency to make a wring boring and ridiculous. For example:

Incorrect	It is not good to treat women in an awful manner. Treating women in an often

manner is just not right. It is just not the right thing to do to treat women wrongly

Correct | It is not good to treat women in an awful manner. Treating women awfully is a sign of lack of respect. It shows that such a person does not understand the value of a woman

How To Avoid Fluff In Writing

The following tips should help you avoid fluff in writing:

- Have a plan to write first and edit later
- Trim paragraphs to be short and precise

Specific Advanced Writing Mistakes

Below are specific advance writing mistakes that are difficult to spot:

American And British English

It is important to know your audience. There are some crucial differences in American and British English. You need to know these differences to be able to provide the right content for the right audience. Below are crucial differences in American and British English you need to notice:

Spellings

American	Holidays
British	Vacations
American	Hood
British	bonnet
American	Apartments
British	Flats
American	Holidays
British	Vacations

Collective Nouns

In American English, collective nouns are singular while they can be singular or plural in British English.

American	The band is playing tonight
British	The band are playing tonight

Past Tense

American	learned
British	learned or learnt
American	dreamed
British	learned or learnt
American	burned
British	burned or burnt

Order of Adjectives

The right order of adjectives in English language is quantity, quality, size, age, shape, color, proper adjective, and qualifier.

Incorrect   I am impressed by that **really new large black antique** car at the end of the road

Correct   I am impressed by that **really large new black antique** car at the end of the road

MCQs: choose the appropriate options from the statements below

I will like to purchase those _____ dresses. (A. four big yellow B. big four yellow)

Answer: A

She is a _____ girl. (A. big tall B. tall big)

Answer: B

Further Versus Farther

These two words are often used interchangeably. However, they are not the same and cannot be used as such. "Further" has to do with a figurative distance while "farther" describe a physical distance. Below are the wrong and proper usages of these two words:

Incorrect   To move **farther** in life, you need to maintain your focus

Correct   To move **further** in life, you need to maintain your focus

Incorrect   The Captain told me that we could not move **further** than the short fence due to security reasons

Correct   The Captain told me that we could not move **farther** than the short fence due to security reasons

MCQs: choose the appropriate options from the statements below

If you complain _____, I am going to shoot you. (A. farther B. further)

Answer: B

Kingsley asked his father how _____ he has to walk. (A. farther B. further)

Answer: A

Clichés

A cliché is an expression that has lost its original meaning or novelty due to being overused. Such expressions once held sway but started becoming boring and irritating because they have been used severally and extensively. Below are examples of clichés and expressions you can use instead of them:

Clichés   only time will tell

Replacement to be unveiled over time

Clichés in the nick of time

Replacement to take place just in time

Clichés lost track of time

Replacement to stop paying attention to time

Number Agreement

Since pronouns are used in place of a noun, there must be an agreement between the number of the noun and the pronoun that is replacing it. A singular pronoun has to replace a singular noun and vice versa. Below are statements that do not show number agreement and their corrections:

Incorrect The cat climbed the tree but **they** stopped at the top of the branch

Correct The cat climbed the tree but **it** stopped at the top of the branch

Incorrect Everyone **are** trying to do what is best for **them**

Correct   Everyone **is** trying to do what is best for **him or her**

Incorrect   Dan and John are here to defend **himself**

Correct   Dan and John are here to defend **themselves**

MCQs: choose the appropriate options from the statements below

John and Billy were so unruly that no one wanted to be _____ friend. (A. her B. their)

Answer: B

Soldiers sacrifice a lot to keep _____ in a good physical condition. (A. themselves B. itself)

Answer: A

Feel Good Versus Feel Well

"Feel well" and "feel good" are often being mistaken to mean the same thing. However, they are not the same. "Feel well" has to do with the state of your health while "feel good" has to do with your state of mind. When you are feeling well, you are physically healthy. However, when you are feeling good, you are happy. Below are some wrong and proper usages of these two phrases:

Incorrect — I went to see my doctor this morning because I was not **feeling good**

Correct — I went to see my doctor this morning because I was not **feeling well**

Incorrect — I **feel well** this morning after enjoying myself at the party last night

Correct — I **feel good** this morning after enjoying myself at the party last night

MCQs: choose the appropriate options from the statements below

Seaman was apparently _____ this morning after he was discharged from the clinic yesterday. (A. feeling well B. feeling good)

Answer: A

The new coach has improved the mood in the dressing room as the players claimed that they are now _____ . (A. feeling good B. feeling well)

Answer: A

Active Voice Versus Passive Voices

In an active voice, the subject acts upon it verb. However, in a passive voice, the subject receives the action of the verb. When the passive voice is used properly, it is correct. However, when it is not used in moderation, it becomes weak and incorrect.

Examples of Active Voice

Monkeys love bananas

The dog threw the bone away

Examples of Passive Voice

Bananas are loved by monkeys

The bone was thrown away by the dog

Wrong usages of Active and Passive Voices

Below are some examples of the wrong usage of active and passive voices and how to remedy them:

Don't use passive voices when you should take responsibility for your actions

Incorrect   An error occurred on your account, but **several attempts were made** to remedy it

Correct   We made an error on your account, but **we have made every attempt** to remedy it

Don't fail to identify the subjects in the clauses

Incorrect   **If there are any suggestions,** I can be reached at the number below

Correct   **If you have any suggestions**, call me at the number below

MCQs: Change the following passive voices to active voices

Was a zoo visited by you? (A. Have you been visiting a zoo? by B. Was you visit a zoo? C. Did you visit a zoo?)

Answer: C

He will be praised very much by you (A. You will praise him very much by B. You will be praising him very much C. You will have to praise him very much)

Answer: A

Except Versus Accept

Students are often guilty of using "accept" when "except" would have been more appropriate and vice versa. "Accept" means to receive something offered or agree with something or someone. On the other hand, "except" means excluding something or someone. Hence, the two words are not synonymous.

Here are some common wrong usages of these words and the appropriate way to use them:

Incorrect   My mother can tolerate any other behavior from me **accept** stealing from others

Correct   My mother can tolerate any other behavior from me **except** stealing from others

Incorrect   I have no doubt that Bob will **except** this beautiful gift

Correct   My mother can tolerate any other behavior from me **except** stealing from others

212

MCQs: Change the following passive voices to active voices

Please, will you ____ my gift? (A. except B. accept)

Answer: B

Every member of the crew were all smiles ____ Harry (A. except B. Accept)

Answer: A

CONCLUSION

The attitude to learn is an attribute that you must never lose. I believe that you have learned a lot of important things that will help you speak and write in English more effectively. However, learning must never end here. As much as this book covered a wide range of grammatical and spelling errors, it does not cover every error in English language. Hence, it is imperative that you continue to seek avenues to learn more and continue to improve.

You don't have to be a native speaker before you can write and communicate effectively in English language. There have been people who have won awards for literary works in English language who were not native speakers. Hence, the only limitation to your efficiency in English grammar is the one you place on yourself. You will only be as good as you want to be.

However, desire is not enough. You have to take deliberate steps to improve yourself every day. Buy books and read quality materials that can improve your speaking and writing. The quality of your life is equivalent to what you do with your resources. Your money and time are two vital resources you have to utilize judiciously. Invest your time and money in activities that will improve your life.

RESOURCES

Abdalhussein, M. H. F. 2015. "Grammatical Error Analysis of Iraqi Postgraduate Students' Academic Writing: The Case of Iraqi Students in UKM Dr. Mohammed Subakir: Universiti Kebangsaan Malaysia". International Journal of Education and Research Vol. 3 No. 6.

Brown, H. D. 2000. Principles of Language Learning and Teaching. (4th Ed.). New York: Addison, Wesley, Longman, Inc.

Ernawati, E. 2010. "Identifying Problems in Students' Final Projects Based on Scientific Guidelines". Jurnal Lingua Cultura, Vol. 4 No.2, 201-217.

Jackson, H. 2005. Good Grammar for Students. London: Sage Publications.

Langacker, R. W. 2008. Cognitive Grammar: A Basic

Introduction. New York: Oxford University Press, Inc.

Purpura, J. E. 2004. Assessing Grammar. Cambridge: Cambridge University Press.

Schauer, G. A. 2009.Interlanguage Pragmatic Development: The Study Abroad Context. London: Continuum International Publishing Group.

Selinker, L. and Gass, S. M. 2008. Second Language Acquisition: An Introductory Course. (3rd Ed.). New York: Routledge.

Sugeng, B., Supriyanti, N., Nurcahyo, R. 2005. Peningkatan Penguasaan Tatabahasa Bahasa Inggris Mahasiswa Jurusan Bahasa Iinggris FBS UNY melalui Pendekatan 'Common Core' yang Telah Dimodifikasi. (Research Report). Yogyakarta: FBS UNY.

Swan, M. 2006. 'Teaching Grammar – Does Grammar Teaching Work?' Modern English Teacher 15/2.

Thornbury, S. 2002. How to Teach Grammar (5th Ed.).

Essex: Pearson Education.

Trousdale, G. and Gisborne, N. (Eds.). 2008.

Constructional Approaches to English Grammar.

New York:

Mouton, the Hague.

Young, D. J. 1984. Introducing English Grammar. London:

Hutchinson Education, Ltd.

Zhang, J. 2009. "Necessity of Grammar Teaching".

International Education Studies 2/2: 184-187.

CPSIA information can be obtained
at www.ICGtesting.com
Printed in the USA
LVHW092127100621
689964LV00009B/58